NEW
GUINEA
an island apart

For Karen

NEW
GUINEA
an island apart

NEIL NIGHTINGALE

BBC Books

Published by BBC Books,
a division of BBC Enterprises Limited,
Woodlands, 80 Wood Lane, London W12 0TT

First published 1992
© Neil Nightingale 1992

ISBN 0 563 36161 1

Designed by Graeme Dudley Associates
Map by Eugene Fleury
Set in Baskerville Roman $12/14\frac{1}{2}$
Printed and bound in Great Britain by Butler & Tanner Ltd, Frome and London
Colour separation by Technik Ltd, Berkhamstead
Jacket printed by Belmont Press Ltd, Northampton

CONTENTS

Picture Credits

ACKNOWLEDGEMENTS

*N*ew Guinea is an island whose natural riches are still being uncovered. This book, and the television programmes which it accompanies, would not have been possible without the generous advice and practical assistance of the many scientists and others who have spent far more time than I have exploring and studying the island, its wildlife and people.

Those to whom I owe special thanks are: Akia Aruah, Chris Bonnie, Ian Burrows, John Chappell, David Coates, Tim Flannery, John Fraser Stewart, Lucy Gilkes, Les Groube, Mike Hopkins, Steve Harvey, Iamo Ila, Bob Johns, Paulus Kulmoi, Roy Mackay, James Menzies, Stephen Nash, Michael O'Hanlon, Mark O'Shea, Terry Reardon, Chris Rose and Lester Seri.

I am also deeply indebted to Matthew Jebb, director of the Christensen Research Institute in Madang, whose enthusiasm for the natural history of New Guinea has been an inspiration throughout, and whose advice, both on the programmes and the book, has been invaluable.

Trans Niugini Tours took our camera teams to many exciting locations and their staff at Ambua, Bensbach and Karawari lodges shared with us their extensive knowledge of the animals, plants and people of the surrounding areas.

Without the support of Mike Salisbury, editor of *The Natural World* television series, neither the films or this book would have been possible. The assistant producer, Phil Chapman, has given me great help over the last year and has steered me away from error on numerous occasions. I spent many enjoyable months in New Guinea in the company of cameraman, Michael Pitts, and sound recordist, Rogier Frederiks. Michael provided the majority of the beautiful images for the films and many of the photographs for this book. Rogier recorded a whole range of wonderful sounds. Alain Compost, Alan Hayward and Kevin Flay also contributed vital film sequences and Jill Garrett edited all the pictures and sounds to create the final programmes.

I am very grateful to Pam Jackson and Liz Toogood for their hard work in Bristol, ensuring that a production operating on the far side of the globe has run smoothly throughout. Pam, Liz, Phil Chapman and Karen Bass all helped me with invaluable comments on an early draft of the manuscript.

For their support, encouragement and advice I also thank Sheila Ableman, Anna Ottewill and Jennifer Fry at BBC Books.

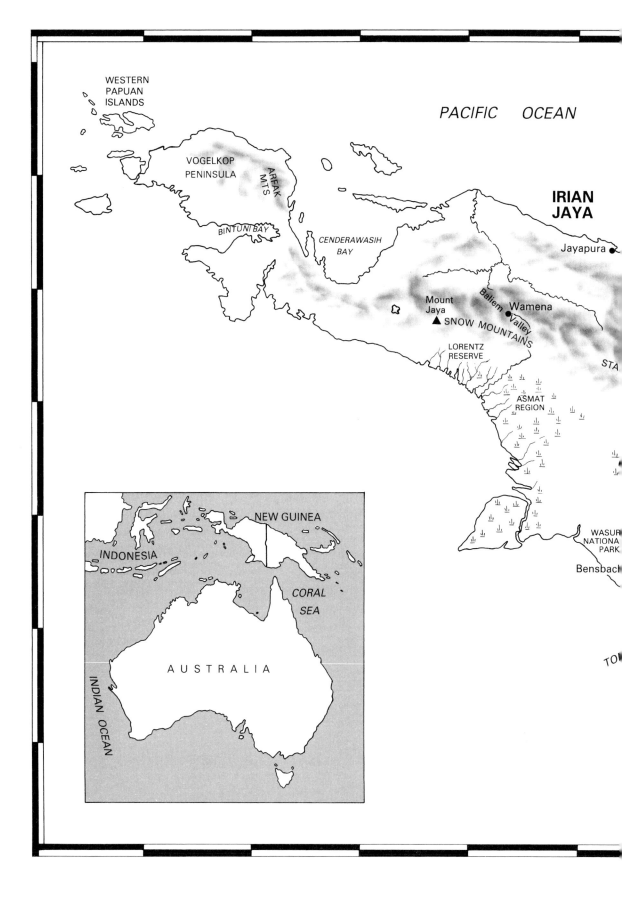

INTRODUCTION

'*A* country which contains more strange and new and beautiful natural objects than any other part of the globe,' was how the famous naturalist Sir Alfred Russell Wallace described New Guinea after visiting it in 1858. Over the past two and a half years I've been fortunate to be able to travel to this fabulous island on several occasions while making two films for the BBC television series *The Natural World*.

As I have discovered on my travels, much of the place remains as it was when Wallace stepped ashore in the middle of the last century. The total land area is about six times the size of England, and over 70 per cent is still clothed in dense tropical forests containing all kinds of bizarre animals and plants. Located between Asia and Australia, New Guinea has received life from both continents. The flora and fauna have colonised habitats that range from coral reefs, through tropical swamps, savannas and forests, to mountain peaks clad in snow and ice. The result – New Guinea contains a phenomenal diversity of life. In spite of this great biological wealth no book has ever been written that describes the natural history of the whole island for non-specialists. This one is intended to fill that gap.

It also links the story of the wildlife, vegetation and landscapes to that of the people and their astounding variety of culture. Their ancestors have been living here and using the natural resources of the island for at least the past 40 000 years.

The main island of New Guinea lies among many smaller ones in the south-west corner of the Pacific. Together they form a geographical area called Melanesia, literally 'black islands' in classical Greek. It is so named because the people tend to be darker skinned than those living elsewhere in the Pacific. The islands nearest New Guinea have close biological links with it and in this book are considered part of it. They include New Britain, New Ireland, the Louisiade archipelago, Woodlark Island and the Trobriand, d'Entrecasteaux, and the Western Papuan islands. These all fall within the political boundaries of the two nations that now share the main island of New Guinea, Papua New Guinea and Indonesia.

The island is split by a line drawn by Europeans in the late nineteenth century across the land, most of which had never been seen by a white man. That legacy continues to affect the island, its people, and even its natural environment and wildlife.

The eastern half of the island was once ruled by Australia and is now the independent country of Papua New Guinea. It's a vibrant, if at times chaotic, democracy with a strong Melanesian cultural identity, tempered by significant western influences. Most scientific research concerning the island has been conducted in Papua New Guinea. Consequently, most books and publications about New Guinea cover only this half.

The western part, once a Dutch colony, is now a province of Indonesia and is called Irian Jaya. Over the past few decades it has been a difficult place for scientists to visit and study. Many areas have been off limits to foreigners, usually for security reasons. The local Melanesian population have not always acquiesced peacefully to domination by a government whose authority comes from far away Jakarta. As a result only a small amount of recent research has been done on the natural history of Irian Jaya. I visited the province for filming and have drawn together a considerable amount of information on it, as well as on Papua New Guinea.

Both halves of New Guinea are changing fast. The entire island contains a fabulous wealth of resources, some already tapped, many more yet to be exploited. Oil, natural gas, gold, copper and timber are now attracting massive foreign investment to one of the world's last wild frontiers. Yet New Guinea is one of only a handful of places left on the planet where there's still an opportunity to save large areas of wilderness, especially large areas of tropical rainforest. The next few decades will reveal whether that exciting opportunity is seized, or lost forever.

Chapter One

ISLAND ALIVE

alking across the white crusty ground near the Pokili hotsprings the heat of the earth can be felt on the feet, even through a decent pair of shoes. It is as though there's a fire beneath the soil. There is. In New Guinea the molten rock inside the planet comes uncomfortably and often violently close to the surface. It's the reason New Guinea and its surrounding islands are here at all.

Pokili lies on one of those offshore islands. It's a place of sulphurous smells, bubbling mud pools and geysers that shoot fountains of water and steam into the air. The regularity with which the geysers blow is curiously related to the state of the tide on the nearby ocean. At first sight they seem to be no more than sinister holes with steeply sloping sides, but wait for several minutes at the right time of day and rumbling and gurgling sounds will stir the air. Suddenly water erupts, leaps high, and then boils fiercely before descending as swiftly as it came.

The exploration of this fascinating area requires great care, an experienced local guide and not a little luck. The rock is thin and not always capable of supporting body weight. Although paths wind between the pools and hissing vents, in the past few years several people have fallen through into the scalding world beneath.

The intense heat and fragile surface would seem to make these places incapable of supporting life. Right on top of the geysers and pools that's certainly true, but just a short distance away from the hottest and most hostile spots the volcanic heat becomes a vital necessity for one particular animal. In the forest not far from the edge of the hotsprings, are burrows in the ground. Not just a few but tens of thousands of them, each about half a metre across. The hotsprings cover an area about the size of a football pitch, but the warm earth stretches for several square kilometres, and so do the holes.

Their owners are not strange reptiles or large burrowing rodents: they are birds, and rather ordinary-looking ones at that. Black, and about the same size and stature as chickens, their only remarkable features are their feet. They are huge and powerful and the birds use them for tunnelling. They give the birds their name, megapode, which means 'big foot' in English. The megapodes dig these tunnels, which may extend for 2 metres or so, not to live in but to lay eggs in. The reason for this odd behaviour is that the volcanically heated soil acts as a giant incubator. The eggs develop at a constant temperature without requiring any further help from the parents.

This site, and a few on other islands, such as Tonga and the Solomons, are the only places in the world where birds use volcanic heat to incubate their eggs. But New Guinea is so unlike the rest of the biological world that such surprises are commonplace here. It lies at a crossroads of life between Asia, Australia and the Pacific. Animals and plants have invaded from all directions and once here have evolved in their own unusual ways. The result is an island teeming with life, with a greater diversity of animals and plants than almost anywhere else on earth. Many are strange and most are unique.

New Guinea has the longest lizards and tallest tropical trees in the world. The largest and most spectacular butterflies on earth flash through these forests on iridescent wings almost 30 cm across. It's home to some of the world's most extraordinary birds: the giant cassowary that can tear a man apart with its claws; pigeons with huge feathery crowns on their heads; and most famous of all, the birds of paradise with their extravagant, almost unbelievably impractical plumage. But perhaps most appealing of all are the bizarre marsupial mammals that have evolved in this island

1 The hotsprings at Pokili (ABOVE) on the island of New Britain are evidence of the great volcanic forces that stir in the rocks below.

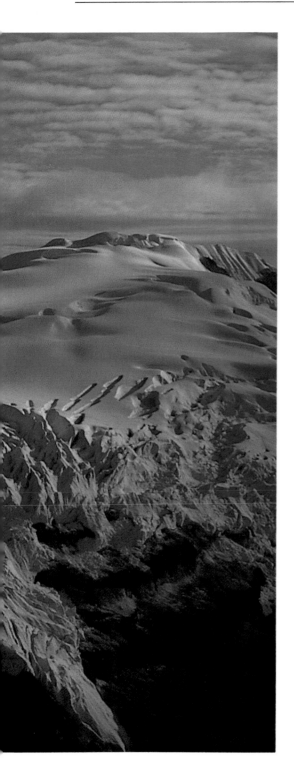

2 PREVIOUS PAGE: *Early morning in the Torricelli Mountains on the north coast of New Guinea.*

3 *New Guinea is the only tropical island high enough to support glaciers on its peaks. Mount Jaya* (LEFT) *reaches an altitude of 4884 metres.*

4 *Just below the summit are long, straight valleys* (ABOVE) *which were carved out by ice at a time when glaciers covered a much greater area of the mountain.*

5 ABOVE: Rainfall in the mountains can be as high as 10 000 millimetres a year, creating lush forests and numerous waterfalls.

6 RIGHT: New Guinea's position, between the Indian and Pacific Oceans, lends itself to one of the richest and most varied coral reefs in the world.

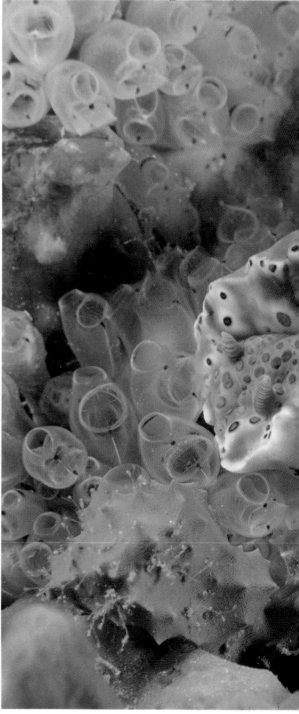

7 PREVIOUS PAGE, LEFT: *Whip gorgonians are amongst the most colourful of all corals. Their polyps catch plankton from the passing currents.*

8 PREVIOUS PAGE, RIGHT: *Shoals of barracuda, many hundred-strong, sweep in over the reef in search of prey.*

9 and 11 *The reef is a riot of colour.
The bright coats of nudibranchs
(*FAR LEFT TOP AND CENTRE*)
warn potential predators away.
These animals often have powerful
stings, or are full of nasty-tasting
chemicals.*

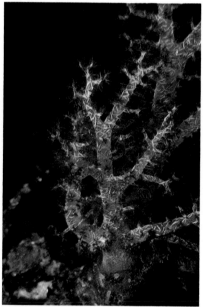

10 *The puffer fish (*FAR LEFT
BELOW*) uses its bold stripes to
signal to other members of its
species.*

12 *It is a mystery why soft corals
(*ABOVE*) such as these are brightly
coloured. They live so far below the
surface that very little light is able
to filter down and, therefore, their
true colours are not naturally visible.*

13 Clown fish (BELOW) *use the stinging tentacles of anemones for protection.*

14 Leatherback turtles (RIGHT) *are the largest turtles in the world. Thousands of females visit the beaches of the Vogelkop Peninsula, each year, to lay their eggs.*

15 OVERLEAF: *The shallow waters around New Guinea are an important refuge for dugongs. Elsewhere in the world they have been hunted, almost to extinction.*

16 *From time to time, violent earthquakes push living reefs up out of the water. This coral island* (ABOVE) *near Madang, was created in such a way.*

isolation. There are no monkeys in the trees. Instead ungainly kangaroos clamber around in the rainforest canopy along with the colourful spotted cuscus, with its pink wrinkled nose, large brown eyes and bare prehensile tail. Others, equally as charming as these, include tiny feather-tailed possums, agile sugar gliders that fly from tree to tree, ferocious little predators called quolls, secretive forest wallabies and the bizarre giant spiny anteater.

The reason the island of New Guinea rose at such an important biological crossroads is that in this corner of the Pacific several great chunks of the earth's outer skin meet. As they have pushed against each other New Guinea has been thrust up at the join until now, at a height of over 4800 metres, it stands as the highest tropical island in the world. The chunks in question are the rocks that make up the continents of Asia and Australia and those that form the seafloor of the Pacific.

Sixty-five million years ago, at the end of the Cretaceous period, the land that now forms the northern mountain ranges of New Guinea was a small string of low-lying islands in a peaceful sea. But by then the great southern super-continent of Gondwanaland was breaking up. It had held together the continents of Australia, Antarctica, Africa and South America, as well as India, Madagascar and Arabia, for well over 200 million years. As the various components slowly drifted apart Australia moved northwards and eventually, about 35 million years ago, struck the rocks on the edge of what is now the Pacific Ocean. In this collision the leading edge of Australia rode up on top of the ocean floor because its rocks were lighter than those of the Pacific, and eventually entangled the low-lying islands to the north. In the hiatus that followed the Asian continent became involved as well. Even today geologists have not sorted out where all the rocks that make up the island have come from.

Because there was so much horizontal movement in the crash great masses of the earth's crust slid over and under each other so now they're completely out of sequence. Rocks from the north now lie further south than rocks originally from the south, and younger rocks that were once on top now lie buried deep beneath much older outcrops. The whole lot has been crumpled and twisted as though it were a sheet of corrugated cardboard, not the many trillion tonnes of planetary surface that it is in reality. As a result New Guinea has some of the most spectacular mountains and most active volcanoes in the world.

The volcanoes are fierce. They are the vents for all that underground energy that is still shunting the earth's crust around in this part of the world. The island of New Britain is built on a chain of over twenty volcanoes that have risen at one of the most active parts of the collision zone. The island has never joined the mainland but lies just north-east of it. Along one edge the sea bed plunges steeply to a depth of over 7 kilometres. Rocks of one crustal plate are being forced under another, and the resulting tension creates the geysers and hotsprings that incubate the megapode eggs. It also creates highly active volcanoes. The number grows from time to time as new eruptions find different routes to the surface.

The newest volcano is Vulcan. It sits in a beautiful inlet called Blanche Bay on the northern tip of New Britain. On its shore lies Rabaul, a small city that has often been called the prettiest little port in the Pacific. Until 1937 Vulcan was a small, low-lying island in the bay. Then, on 28 May of that year, the inhabitants of Rabaul began to feel earth tremors. The seafloor began to rise, lifting a small cargo steamer anchored in the bay right out of the water. Next morning the sea was seething. The water bubbled and shoals of dead fish rose to the surface.

As hundreds of people watched, Vulcan suddenly exploded. It shot a huge column of black ash and pumice over 1000 metres into the air. The blasts continued, building a massive and menacing cloud 10 kilometres high. Within the cloud electrical energy, caused by thousands of tonnes of pumice fragments grating against each other, created powerful sheets of lightning and deafening claps of thunder. And then the destruction began. Tonne upon tonne of hot ash and pumice rained down on the bay, town and surrounding countryside. It continued for several days. People sheltered as best they could – in huts, caves, even churches – but over 500 were killed. They were burnt, suffocated, and buried by the deadly shower of volcanic fallout.

With each convulsion Vulcan added more and more rock to its flanks until it stood, no longer a low-lying island, but a 225 metre high volcano attached to the shoreline. The town of Rabaul took many years to recover and to this day regularly feels the earth shake beneath it.

Vulcan is only one of dozens of volcanoes along New Guinea's northern edge. That eruption in 1937, although destructive, was as nothing compared with some of the volcanic events of the past few hundred years. A few have been so powerful and extensive in their effects that the traditional legends of people far away in the highlands of the interior tell of the havoc they have created. These legends frequently recall a 'time of darkness' when the sun was obscured for days on end and the land showered with ash. These were evidently desperate times for the stories record how crops were buried and people and animals starved.

One particular set of legends seems to relate to an eruption about 300 years ago, according to scientist Russell Blong. He has traced not only the stories but also the ash deposits left behind by this event. They cover a huge area of about 80 000 square kilometres. Calculations reveal that the volcano responsible must have thrown out 10 cubic kilometres of the material. That must have been quite an explosion. In fact it was one of the most powerful and destructive to have taken place anywhere on earth for the past thousand years. It may even have been greater than the famous eruption of Krakatoa which occurred in neighbouring Indonesia in 1883.

Volcanic eruptions are so destructive in this part of the world because they involve a highly viscous form of magma called andesite. In locations like Hawaii, where ocean floor is still being created, relatively fluid rock oozes up to the surface. This basalt, as it is called, may look spectacular as it flows down the flank of the island or cascades from the mouth of a volcanic crater, but because it flows so freely it is much less dangerous than andesite. Where ocean floor is being destroyed, as it is in the trenches around New Guinea, volcanic eruptions involve a very different process. As the oceanic and continental rocks grind against each other, deep in the trench their surfaces experience intense heat and pressure, and begin to melt. Water becomes mixed in as well and some of the molten magma is transformed into a new type of rock – andesite. This begins to rise, powered by heat and gases trapped within it, but because it is viscous, does so very slowly. During a volcanic eruption, when those pent-up gases are trying to escape, it resists being thrust to the surface. As pressure builds up within the earth the andesite acts rather like a cork in a champagne bottle. Eventually the strain becomes too great and the volcano bursts open with enormous destructive power.

Today the volcano responsible for those 'time of darkness' legends lies quietly off the shore of northern New Guinea near the town of Madang. Its name is Long Island, and from the sea there is little sign that it once gave a massive demonstration of the earth's explosive power. But a flight over the island reveals the secrets of its past. During the explosion the centre of the volcano was blown apart, creating a cauldron-like crater, a classic caldera.

From inside, the sheer scale of the volcano becomes apparent. The crater is over 10 kilometres wide and has walls that plunge vertically for several hundred metres into the waters of a lake. It is a grim and lonely place, isolated from the rest of the world. Turbulent winds sweep the surface of the lake and no fish swim below. Patches of water regularly heat up to unbearable temperatures. At its centre is a small grey island called Motmot. This is no ordinary island, but a miniature volcano that appeared as the result of an eruption in 1968. The water along the shoreline is scalding to the touch and the sand on its edge steams, as moisture is expelled by underground volcanic heat. Only a few small shrubs have colonised its grey lava slopes. Any life that does survive here does so precariously because Motmot could belch more molten rock at any moment.

Because most of New Guinea's active volcanoes are associated with ocean trenches, they are, like Long Island, mainly off the coast. In an area as geologically complex as this, however, every rule has its exception. For the people of Higaturu village near Mount Lamington that exception came in 1951. Although Mount Lamington is on the mainland, its explosion was one of the most deadly this century. Superheated gases built up under great pressure within the volcano, trapped by a plug of viscous andesite. With little warning the plug burst and an avalanche of fiery gas, mixed with molten rock and ash, shot down the mountainside at nearly 100 kilometres an hour, killing about 3000 people.

On the mainland most of the remaining volcanoes are quiescent. It is as though the rocks have jammed against each other so hard that they are stuck. Over the past ten to fifteen million years, these rocks have created not only volcanoes but also towering mountains. New Guinea must be one of the steepest, most rugged areas of land in the world. It has been thrust so high that glaciers sit on its peaks. The mountains rise so steeply that you can stand in glacial snow and ice at a height of over 4800 metres and look down on blue tropical seas only 100 kilometres away on the coast.

Some of the island's rocks are still rising today. There is no more dramatic evidence of that than on the Huon Peninsula. This is a mountainous spur of land that juts out from the north coast towards New Britain. Along a stretch of its shore the grassy hills rise in a flight of spectacular terraces, rather like a broad staircase some 80 kilometres wide. The massive steps rise to a height of over 600 metres. Each terrace was once a submerged coral reef. Whole coral heads jut out of the hillside to prove the point. The preservation of some has been so good that individual species can be identified.

In a series of vertical shunts the reefs have been lifted clean out of the water and pushed skyward. This has been going on for hundreds of thousands of years and is still happening today. The Huon coastline is rising about 3–4 centimetres every 100 years. That may not sound much but it makes this some of the fastest rising rock in the world. If it continued at the same speed the coral would rise almost as high as the tallest mountains on the island in just over a million years, a blink of an eye on the geological time scale.

Because this area of the island has been the site of such dramatic uplifting, the mountains in the interior of the Huon Peninsula rise very high, to over 4000 metres. As they have risen they have been just as dramatically carved up by rivers descending to the sea. Even those grassy terraces are deeply dissected by steep ravines and gullies. Because this etching has happened so recently the sharp edges have not been rounded off by the slow erosion of wind and water. The result is a landscape of steep V-shaped valleys and razor-sharp ridges, fast-flowing rivers, and dramatic waterfalls.

To the south it is divided from the rest of the island by a broad, straight valley carrying the Markham river. It was along this line that the rocks of Australia collided with those Pacific islands millions of years ago. It is the force of that collision that is still thrusting the land on the Huon Peninsula upwards.

All this recent mountain building has created many barriers across the country, isolating one part from another. That has encouraged the evolution of differing forms of life in each separate part. The Huon Peninsula is no exception. There are, for example, at least three birds of paradise found here and nowhere else: the Huon astrapia, the Emperor bird of paradise, and Wahnes' parotia. The first two live in the forest canopy and the males display in the tree tops to attract females. The call of the male Emperor is reputed to be the most varied and musical of any bird of paradise. In contrast to these two, Wahnes' parotia constructs a display ground on the forest floor. The male is a startling bird. He is black all over except for a bright iridescent breast, a tuft of golden feathers above his beak and a tiny patch of blue at the back of his neck. But most striking of all are the six wire-like plumes that shoot out from behind his eyes. At the end of each they splay out into a tiny disc. The male displays vigorously on the prepared ground, waving those wire plumes so violently that they seem to have a life of their own. Females, presumably, find this irresistible.

All along the north coast are isolated mountain ranges each with their own unique varieties of animals and plants. The Torricelli Mountains, for example, have their own species of tree kangaroo that was only discovered in 1987. In the mountains of the Vogelkop Peninsula in Irian Jaya there are several birdwing butterflies that occur nowhere else on the island, as well as a number of unique birds, such as the Arfak astrapia, western parotia, Vogelkop bowerbird and the Vogelkop scrub wren.

Former mountain peaks that now stand off the coast as islands also support their own special animals. Wilson's bird of paradise and the red bird of paradise are restricted to the Western Papuan Islands. Fergusson Island, off the east coast, has its own type of striped possum, while nearby Woodlark Island has a unique species of cuscus, a marsupial related to possums. This isolation of species on mountain ranges, even on a single mountain top or in a specific valley, has been just one way in which the rugged landscape has influenced the evolution of the fauna and flora.

The mountains are the single most important and impressive element in the island's geology. To anyone who visits New Guinea they are likely to be one of their most memorable and exciting experiences, especially from the air. Many of the planes that service the smaller towns have no radar, and heading into the cloud-covered mountains of the interior is quite exhilarating.

At lower altitudes the clouds hang down in drapes, grey and murky. They obscure the true height and size of the mountains. But once above them in a plane they seem to become mountains themselves – living ones, sucking up moisture from the forest below, bubbling and churning under the driving force of the intense tropical sun. Flying between these great peaks of moving cloud you are acutely aware that behind any one of the curtains of white there could be a solid wall of rock. Many a light plane in New Guinea has entered an innocent-looking cloud never to appear on the other side.

The central spine of the island is a complex system of mountain chains and upland valleys that stretches for nearly 2000 kilometres. At either end it is less than 50 kilometres wide but in the centre expands to a width of about 200 kilometres. In parts low foothills flank the main cordillera, but on the southern flank, near the border between Irian Jaya and Papua New Guinea, the slopes rise over 4000 metres in only 15 kilometres. Towering cliffs, such as the Hindenburg Wall, rise sheer for over 1000 metres.

On the rare days when visibility is near perfect you can look down over the peaks of the Star Mountains onto steep slopes that fall dramatically to either side of the island. To the south they meet the vast floodplain of the Fly River, and to the north the flat expanse of land crossed by the Sepik River. The headwaters of these, the two greatest rivers in New Guinea, arise only a few kilometres apart.

The nature of the mountains depends very much on the under-lying rocks from which they are made. Most are sedimentary rocks laid down as mudstones, sandstones, siltstones or limestones in ancient seas, and thrust up to these heights only in the past few million years. Being so recently risen, erosion has not yet had the chance to round them off. They stand as sharp crested ridges and irregular V-shaped valleys with steep slopes. In some areas of limestone they have been even more dramatically shaped. Lime-stone is soluble in water and over thousands of years rainwater can etch into it and carve spectacular landscapes.

In places these consist of huge caves that extend for unknown distances underground, often carrying large rivers. One of the biggest 'disappearing rivers' in the world, the Baliem, flows through the Irian Jaya highlands near Wamena. It is about 100 metres across but suddenly ends in a massive and turbulent whirlpool up against a wall of limestone. The river literally sinks down into the ground. In several locations water has worn away caves so wide that their roofs have completely collapsed, letting in light and creating gaping holes in the landscape.

Over some areas the erosion has been even more extensive, creating whole hillsides of spire-like towers and steep pyramids, interspersed with deep holes. This is called karst and is almost totally impenetrable to mankind. Near the Baliem River an extensive plateau of cone karst stretches for several kilometres like a giant, upturned egg tray. The southern highlands of Papua New Guinea also have spectacular karst scenery. Close to Lake Kutubu the rock is covered with a blanket of thick vegetation, but just north of Tari most is bare rock. Both the horizontal and vertical edges are razor sharp, and sprout needle-like projections. The odd stunted bush clings to sheer walls of limestone that plunge into deep vegetated depressions. There are no rivers or streams in a landscape like this. The water simply drains away vertically, into the rock itself, to coalesce and form underground waterways which eventually emerge as springs in the valleys below.

The high rainfall in these mountains has been vital in the creation of such dramatic landscapes. It has also given the island an almost incalculable number of spectacular waterfalls. On steep cliffs sheets of water often seem to spring directly from the rock itself. The rainfall is so heavy that rocky walls, normally dry, often become veiled in an almost continuous curtain of falling spray. Where large rivers are involved the effect is even more impressive. The Beaver Falls are a whole series of crescents and cascades, while the Wawoi Falls are a gently curving miniature Niagara set among luxuriantly forested slopes.

The weather is a product of the mountains and in New Guinea this is particularly so. This is one of the wettest places on earth. Some parts of the island receive almost daily rainfall and a yearly average of over 10 000 millimetres. That is about ten times more rain than falls in Great Britain. The mountains trap the warm, moist air of the equatorial winds. From December to April the north-west monsoon blows, and from May to October the prevailing winds are the south-east trades. As they rise up over the mountains they cool, their water condenses, builds clouds and eventually falls as rain. In the mountains themselves the climate does not vary much throughout the year. There are simply times when it is a little less wet than usual. In the shadow of the mountains, however, there is often a distinct dry season, especially in the south of the island where conditions are savanna-like.

On the highest mountains precipitation falls as snow, in spite of the fact that they are little more than 400 kilometres from the equator. With each 300 metre gain in altitude, temperatures generally drop by about 2°C. On the highest mountains this is sufficient to ensure that temperatures regularly fall below zero. Frosts form and lakes ice over. On the very tallest peaks the weather is cold enough to maintain glaciers some 40 metres thick.

New Guinea's highest peak is Mount Jaya in Irian Jaya, at 4884 metres – that's over 16 000 feet. Its top is bare rock but on the slope below there are thick sheets of ice and snow. Today they cover an area of only about four or five square kilometres but in the past they were much larger. Since the middle of the last century world climate has been slowly warming and the ice has been retreating.

As the mountains rise from the coast up to this height they pass through a variety of habitats. Different plants have adapted to the specific conditions of temperature and rainfall at each altitude, so that the island contains almost every type of environment except deserts. This is yet another way in which those great geological forces which created the island have contributed to the enormous variety of life that now lives here.

Just below the ice caps grow plants that would be familiar to Arctic botanists. The vegetation is tundra-like, consisting of ground-hugging mosses and lichens. Further afield bogs and fens cover the landscape. Lower down, the shrubs become taller and eventually the scenery becomes dotted with tree ferns. A thick carpet of grasses, lichens, tree ferns and herbs cover the ground. Below these alpine grasslands gnarled and stunted trees begin to appear and the slopes take on a patchwork appearance. Open areas are interspersed with woodlands draped in moss. This is the start of the cloud forest.

The various bands of plant life at different altitudes reveal a great deal about the history of the island. Many of the small alpine plants have their nearest relations in the Himalayas 5000 kilometres away, while slightly lower down, the tree ferns are remnants of Gondwanaland, the great southern continent. Plants related to those in Asia must presumably have dispersed as seeds across the ocean because New Guinea has never been physically connected to Asia. The Gondwanan species may have rafted on the fragments of that supercontinent, to pop up today in New Guinea, Australia, New Zealand, Africa and South America.

Descending even lower, the flora is definitely Gondwanan in ancestry. Southern beeches, almost identical with those in New Zealand, predominate. Epiphytes drip from every branch and fallen tree, and tree ferns sprout in the understorey. The forest is more often than not shrouded in mist. Moisture clings to every surface. This is the mid-montane forest. Slightly lower down, trees appear from a family that very definitely has its origins in the opposite direction – the oaks.

Below these mountain forests the trees become taller and more typical of tropical rainforest. The number of plant species increases dramatically. Many are related to species found in Asian rainforests. Eventually, on and around the floodplains of the great rivers, the trees become truly gigantic, with large crowns rising to 50 metres in height. Huge buttress roots support their weight. In the more waterlogged areas pandans and sago trees survive more successfully than those of the rainforest. On the vast floodplains of southern New Guinea seasonally flooded savanna supports paper bark and eucalyptus woodlands. Finally, in estuaries and along the coast, mangroves take over.

From swamps, savanna and tropical rainforest, up sheer escarpments with tumbling waterfalls, to mountains clad with cloud forest, alpine meadows, tundra and ice, New Guinea has a greater variety of different habitats than almost any similar sized piece of land in the world. In each grow different plants that in turn support collections of different animals. In addition to this, each separate mountain range has its own assortment of animals and plants that have evolved in isolation from the others. Combine that with New Guinea's position between Asia and Australia, from both of which it has received a selection of life, and it's clear why this one island has a diversity of animals and plants that beats almost any other place on earth.

Chapter Two

UNDERWATER WEALTH

*O*n the barrier reef at Madang, on the north coast of New Guinea, is a gaping hole in the coral, a great breach through which the nutrient rich waters of the lagoon flow out to meet the clear deep blue of the Pacific Ocean. Its walls rise sheer from the sandy bottom at 30 metres and end only an arm's length from the surface. Near the top of the reef the gap is about 50 metres wide and, with the current flowing fast, a swimmer can be swept its entire length in little more than a minute. It is called Magic Passage. The reasons for its name become immediately and spectacularly apparent if you dive through it.

At the surface swim shoals of giant hump-headed parrot fish, each nearly a metre long. As they eat the living coral they emit great clouds of limestone waste which trails behind them. Smaller but much prettier fish dart along the walls of the reef. Their names alone reveal the strange variety of life that finds a home here: long-nosed butterfly fish, masked banner fish, unicorn surgeon fish, scribbled puffer fish and masked monocled bream. In the brightly lit waters near the surface the corals themselves are a riot of colour and variety: branching staghorns, domes of convoluted brain coral, the soft waving fronds of leather coral, round plates of mushroom coral, and mounds of stumpy porites.

At around 15 metres purple and red sea fans sprout from the

walls of the Passage, spreading their tentacles to filter prey from the passing current. They belong to a group of soft corals called gorgonians. Beside them stand giant barrel sponges, each the size of a man. A variety of large anemones and their attendant anemone fish are also common at this depth. Their tentacles sweep back and forth in the turbulent underwater hurricane that blows from one end of the Passage to the other.

In the deepest parts grow the most beautiful corals of all: exquisitely translucent colonies with soft white stems and delicate pink polyps. Down here ugly-looking groupers hang motionless just above the sea bed, and parties of barracuda and jacks patrol in search of food. Sharks often sweep in at great speed and then disappear in a flash, back into the deep blue of the open ocean.

Even the sandy floor is carpeted with life: crabs, spiny lobsters, pistol shrimps, a variety of shellfish, and, most conspicuous of all, thousands of garden eels. Each is about a metre long and has its hind end in a burrow. From the burrow the rest of the body stands vertical in the water and ends in a tiny pair of eyes and a mouth. As a group they stretch across the sand like a field of underwater corn waving gently in the breeze. Their breeze is the current. It carries small particles of food which they snatch and swallow. At the slightest sight of danger, and that includes a diver passing overhead, they all slither back down into their holes in unison, and in less than a second.

The reason that Magic Passage has such a rich variety of fish and other marine life is because of the currents that flow here. The rich, soupy water of the lagoon is channelled out this way and a great abundance of filter-feeding animals take advantage of this. They in turn attract fish and other animals that feed on them. But the currents do not only bring food. The waters from the open ocean and from the lagoon meet at this point and bring with them animals from each of these different worlds. In these waters swim the tiny larvae that will one day grow into the fish, crabs, shrimps, worms, sea urchins and all the other animals that bring colour and activity to a reef. On a larger scale, ocean currents from many directions carry larvae to settle on all the myriad islands, atolls, and fringing, barrier and patch reefs that surround the coasts of New Guinea.

With such a high concentration of animals on any area of reef competition is severe and the first priority for every living organism is to avoid being eaten. That's exceptionally difficult on the reef because not everything is what it seems. A lump of coral draped in algae may turn out to be a hungry lion fish, and a rock might really be a venomous stonefish in disguise. The most common way for smaller animals to avoid surprise attack from larger ones is to use camouflage too. With such a diversity of different corals, not to mention all the various kinds of weed, it's impossible to be invisible against every background. The solution is to specialise, and no group of animals does this better than the nudibranchs or, as they are sometimes called, the seaslugs. Although related to slugs, their variety of often vivid colours makes them truly beautiful animals. They cruise over the sea bed or swim through the water, gently rippling their bodies as if in an underwater ballet.

The Madang Lagoon holds the world record, over six hundred species of nudibranchs. For almost every kind of soft coral, sponge and weed there seems to be a nudibranch to match. They match not only in colour but in texture and shape too. If a coral has little bumps on then so does its matching seaslug. Some grow their gills into shapes that resemble coral polyps. Another species lives on weed which has tiny bubble bladders on its fronds. It too has grown a collection of spherical bubbles on its back to complete the disguise.

Other nudibranchs opt for a different strategy. They go all out to advertise their presence with gaudy coats of bright reds and yellows, black and orange stripes, or vivid purple spots. At first this may seem suicidal but there is method in this apparently mad colouring. Some of these particular seaslugs contain noxious substances in their skin, often derived from their prey. Holding one of these creatures out of water, the smell of terpenes or other nasty chemicals can be pretty overpowering, and they must taste awful.

The Aeolid nudibranchs, also brightly coloured, use another type of defence. They feed on coelenterates such as soft corals or hydroids. These have a defence system of stinging cells called nematocysts, but the nudibranchs can eat them with impunity. In fact they swallow the nematocysts intact and then transport them within their body to the surface of their own skin. Here they function as though they were still in the coelenterate. Any predator biting the seaslug receives a painful sting in the mouth. Fish who have made this mistake spit out their intended prey. Their lips often quiver in apparent discomfort, and they soon learn to avoid that particular type of nudibranch. The bright and distinctive colours advertise the danger, whether chemical or physical. They warn most fish away and ensure that if they do attack they do not make the same mistake again.

In this crowded world of disguise and deceit other animals hijack this defence system for their own benefit. Many entirely harmless worms adopt the same bright colours as seaslugs to ward off predators who are unable to tell the difference between real danger and bluff. Of course, if a particular fish has not learnt the system the colours in themselves will provide no protection at all.

Worms are not the only animals to try this ploy. Eels do it too. They are entirely inoffensive but one species mimics a very distinctive black and white seasnake that is highly poisonous. Naturally, potential predators cannot afford to tangle with an animal that might just turn out to be deadly. The eel even swims in a way which exactly mimics the snake's movements, and has a modified and flattened tail so that its body shape also matches precisely. But there is a final twist in the tale. The only animal that can tell that the eel is not a snake is the snake itself. So, ironically, the real snake preys on the eel that stole its colours.

Some animals rely directly on others to provide them with active protection. Sea anemones provide a favourite home for certain fish, crabs and shrimps because their stinging tentacles deter predators. The Madang Lagoon has a staggering variety of anemones and their partners. Fish are the most familiar. There are several different species, each specialising in sharing its life with a particular type of anemone. At an early age the fish develop a protective chemical signal on their coat which prevents the anemone from mistakenly stinging them to death. When danger approaches they dart right in among the deadly tentacles, even into the anemone's mouth and stomach.

In this underwater jungle many of the familiar stories from on land are played out, but with a different cast. In Africa or South America if an animal shakes or in any way molests an acacia tree hordes of ants swarm out to defend it. In return for this protection service the plant provides the ants with food and a home inside a special gall. On the New Guinea reefs the trees are replaced by branching corals and the ants by *Trapezia* crabs. These tiny little crabs come in a variety of colours – pinks and blues, purples and reds. Many are conspicuously spotted. Each lives on a specific type of coral, feeding on the mucus it produces. This is all the food a crab requires and it will remain among the branches of a single coral for its entire life. In return, when any animal appears looking for a coral meal, the crab rushes out and attacks. It can even ward off the voracious crown of thorns starfish, a creature that elsewhere has created havoc by consuming large areas of the Great Barrier Reef. Such a tiny crab, no larger than a thumbnail, can have a crucial part to play in preserving the whole reef, and hence the many other animals that depend on it. The same is true of many of the intimate interactions which at first sight seem so bizarre and esoteric. The reef's stability is tied into them all and even the smallest disturbance can, through a chain reaction, upset the ecological balance of the entire community of animals and plants.

The joy of diving on New Guinea's coral is that not only does it support a huge variety of life but that the reef structures themselves are also incredibly varied. Unlike the Great Barrier Reef, which lies just a few hundred kilometres further south, these reefs grow close to the shore. Within quite a small area, and within easy boating distance, you can explore the sunlit world of a shallow patch reef or follow a towering wall of coral into the depths. You can swim in huge caves, through narrow clefts, around palm-fringed coral islands, or across calm lagoons, all in a single afternoon.

The complex geological formations which created a whole range of different substrates on which coral can grow, and the various sea level changes over the past few million years are the reasons for this diversity. The distribution of such underwater coral landscapes also depends crucially on the biology of the reefs themselves, because that determines the depth to which they can grow.

Some corals can grow down to about 80 metres but many require much shallower water than that. They need light for the tiny symbiotic algae which live within them, and sunlight drops off dramatically with increased depth. These algae, called zooxanthellae, allow corals to grow much faster and larger than they

17 The extensive rainforests of New Guinea contain no monkeys or apes. Instead, they support a whole range of marsupial possums, including the spotted cuscus (ABOVE).

18 LEFT: *Goodfellow's tree kangaroo. The kangaroo's body design is intended for hopping around on the ground. However, in New Guinea several species have evolved to live up in the canopy of the forest.*

19 ABOVE: *Another marsupial, the sugar glider, uses flaps of skin on the sides of its body to glide from one tree to the next in search of sap, gum and nectar.*

20 ABOVE: *The quoll is the largest marsupial predator on the island. About the size of a small domestic cat, it feeds on birds, reptiles, small mammals and insects.*

21 BELOW: *The diet of the unusual long-beaked echidna consists mainly of earthworms, which it sucks up through its long snout.*

22 PREVIOUS PAGE RIGHT: *The rich supply of forest fruit supports huge numbers of fruit bats. These are bare-backed fruit bats departing from their roost.*

*23 Blossom bats (*ABOVE*) feed on nectar and pollen and are amongst the most important flower pollinators in the rainforest.*

*24, 25 and 26 The vast majority of the world's 43 species of birds of paradise are found only in the forests of New Guinea. In the superb (*ABOVE*), the king (*ABOVE*

RIGHT) *and the blue birds of*
paradise (BELOW RIGHT)*, as in*
most other species, it is the males
who are the showiest and most
colourful of the sexes.

27, 28 and 29 *Bright colour seems to be a characteristic of many types of rainforest bird. A raggiana bird of paradise (**PREVIOUS PAGE ABOVE LEFT**), a superb fruit dove (**PREVIOUS PAGE BELOW LEFT**), and a group of rainbow lorikeets (**PREVIOUS PAGE RIGHT**).*

30, 31 and 32 *The rainforests of New Guinea* (BELOW) *look just like those found in the rest of the world but the animals which live within them are quite different. They support no large carnivores and, as a result, several ground-living birds have evolved. The crowned pigeon* (LEFT) *can fly short distances, if threatened, but the cassowary* (CENTRE) *is entirely flightless. Cassowaries nest on the forest floor and the males guard the eggs and then protect the young for several months after hatching.*

33 PREVIOUS PAGE: Perpetual mist in the air encourages mosses, ferns and many other epiphytic plants to sprout from the trunks and branches of forest trees.

34 and 37 High humidity is a necessary condition for the growth of forest fungi (ABOVE). A damp environment is also ideal for the many different kinds of frog that live in these rainforests. BELOW RIGHT: the green tree frog.

35 and 36 The Hercules moth
(**LEFT**) *is the largest moth in the
world with a wing span of about 25
centimetres. Its caterpillar
(**ABOVE**) is spectacularly coloured.*

38 While resting, green tree pythons (ABOVE) have a very characteristic way of folding their coils.

39 White-tailed paradise kingfishers (TOP) have unusual nests built in termite mounds on the forest floor. This one is just leaving its nest.

otherwise would. Not all species of coral possess such partners but those that do not are unable to form large colonies or build extensive reefs.

As a result of photosynthesis the zooxanthellae produce oxygen and carbohydrates which the coral can collect and use. In some cases the algae supply up to 98 per cent of all the food that the coral requires and they also help it deposit calcium. This enables corals to build their limestone skeletons three times faster in sunlight than in darkness. Without their help most reefs would not be able to grow sufficiently quickly to overcome the destructive effects of waves and other erosion. In return for this assistance the algal cells use the waste products of the coral's own body chemistry. This close relationship between coral and algae is the reason that corals have been such a success as master builders.

For a reef to start growing it requires a suitable area of sea bottom at the right depth. Once started, and although it has the help of the algae, the coral can grow upwards only at a certain rate. Some species can increase by as much as 20 centimetres a year, others no more than a few millimetres. If the rock on which they are living is subsiding, or if sea levels in the area are rising, the coral may not be able to keep up. As both have happened on many occasions around the shores of New Guinea the underwater landscape is a patchwork of living coral and areas where the coral has either never started or has subsequently drowned.

Cenderawasih Bay in north-west Irian Jaya is a splendid example of how the underlying geology can create a wonderful assortment of different reefs. It is also a wonderful place to dive, because the scenery around the bay is stunning. The rugged mountains on the edge of the bay are clad in lush tropical forest. Along most of the shore they tumble precipitously into the sea. Growing out from the coast is a narrow rim of coral. Known as fringing reefs, these extend along the base of the coastal cliffs for hundreds of kilometres. Some shelve gently away from the shore while others plunge almost vertically for 40 or 50 metres into the depths.

Along the boundary of geological collision between the mountains of the bay's western coastline and chunks of the Pacific's sea floor is a complex series of geological faults that have created a beautiful chain of islands called the Kepulauan Auri. Each island is surrounded by a necklace of coral. But these are not fringing reefs. The islands themselves are entirely made of coral and once were all submerged.

The coral probably first began to grow on the cones of underwater volcanoes that erupted along the fault line. As sea levels rose and the volcanoes subsided, the coral was able to build and build to keep within the required depth for growth. Some of these reefs are still submerged today and form a shallow platform surrounded by deep water. Others have grown in the shape of a hollow ring. On their seaward side the water is deep but inside they enclose a shallow lagoon. These are classic coral atolls. Yet others have parts that now stand above the waterline and form islands covered in vegetation. Only around their edges, as the reef dips down to the ocean floor, are the corals submerged and hence alive. To add to this variety of underwater geography many of the reefs are dissected by clefts and punctured by caves.

The diversity of landscapes in Cenderawasih Bay is reflected in the diversity of life that inhabits these waters. It is such an important site that the Indonesian government has declared it a marine nature reserve. Over 145 species of reef-building corals live in the bay. Above them butterfly fish, angelfish, damselfish, blennies, puffers and gobies dart and glide in a changing collage of colour. In the deeper, clearer water of the reef edge great shoals of blue and yellow fish called fusiliers twist and turn together. If a diver is really lucky a manta or spotted eagle ray may swoop overhead.

In among the nooks and crannies camouflaged surprises await the well-trained eye. A gentle convulsion may give away the location of a giant clam. This bay is one of the best sites in the world for them. It contains five different species. The largest of all may be a century old and measure a metre across. But in spite of their size they are often difficult to spot nestled in among, and partly overgrown by, coral. While their mouths are open the fleshy blue-green mantle hangs out over the shell and looks just like another bit of reef. This is perhaps not a coincidence because the greenish colour comes from the same kind of algae that live in the coral itself. The giant clams cultivate zooxanthellae for the very same reason that the corals do. They provide extra nutrients for the clams, which may be one of the reasons they are able to grow so large.

In sheer numbers, and in the drama of daily life, the reefs of New Guinea must exceed in spectacle even the teeming plains of Africa. But here, unlike any terrestrial location or even the more frequently dived waters of the world, places can be explored that have probably never been seen by any other person before. Some of the best known locations will, of course, have been visited many times but, with thousands of square kilometres of ocean dotted with islands and coral reefs, the waters of New Guinea have plenty of secrets yet to be uncovered.

To understand the life of the reef and all its intricate connections in full it is vital to observe it not only as the lively colourful world it is during the day but also as the more ominous and eerie place it becomes when the light fails. As the sun dips towards the horizon the waters around the reef turn from a sparkling blue to mottled hues of grey. It is hard to distinguish fish from the background of coral, and even harder to identify them as friend or foe. In this confusing light the predators of the reef change in mood, becoming more aggressive. Tuna, barracuda and sharks all take advantage of the conditions at this time of the day, and launch their last attacks before darkness descends.

Just before sunset the reef suddenly becomes quiet. The daytime fish have finally found a hole or a crevice in which to spend the night and those that prowl only by night have yet to leave their lairs. Large predators still glide silently by, but all their prey has gone. This distinct changeover period on the reef happens for two reasons. First, it is simply a dangerous time to be around: fish that venture out are likely to be eaten. But the physiology of fish eyes also plays a part. Until the sun is completely down there is actually too much light for the highly sensitive eyes of nocturnal fish to be maximally effective. It is not yet dim enough to give them an advantage over potential enemies. Making a move too soon could result in instant death.

Squirrel fish have such eyes. Although they are actually predators, they hide in caves and crevices until night falls for there are plenty of even larger carnivores that could take them as a tasty meal. Their large eyes are not their only adaptation for hunting at night or in the gloom of underwater caverns: surprisingly, their red colour is also used. In the sun this would be highly conspicuous but as light passes through water the red wavelengths are filtered out first. This effect is especially pronounced when there is very little light. In near darkness red colours underwater appear as grey or black, giving the fish the best possible camouflage.

Other fish have a completely different approach to nocturnal hunting and hiding. Descending at night to the bottom of the Madang Lagoon, your lights may pick out the eerie hulk of a wreck, a freighter that was scuttled in the 1970s. It might seem lifeless, but if the diving torches are turned away the portholes of the ship come alive with light of their own. Not just a general illumination but dozens of flashing lamps. At times like this, at 30 metres below the surface, and dwarfed by a great metal monument to a past tragedy, it may be difficult to hang on to your sanity and put aside the thought of mariners' ghosts haunting the stricken ship. But approaching closer, you see that the sources of all the lights come from the harmless flashlight fish, of the genus *Anomalops*.

Beneath their large round eyes each fish has a light-producing organ. It is filled with luminescent bacteria which the fish can apparently control. The bacteria generate the light by a series of chemical reactions. The light is switched on and off when the fish rotates the organ in and out of a special socket. Whether the flashlight fish actually use the light to see better in the dark is a matter of debate. It is more likely to be a device for use against predators. They swim in a school and flash their lights on and off intermittently before suddenly changing direction. This is likely to confuse any hunter trying to catch a specific individual. Other flashlight fish, of the genus *Photoblepheron*, also live in the lagoon and they use their luminescent organs to entice prey towards them. Whatever functions these fish put their lamps to it makes for a strange and fascinating experience to watch the display of a whole school framed through the portholes of a wreck.

On the seafloor at Pig Point, an underwater promontory about half a kilometre from the wreck, curious little creatures sprout from the sand. No more than 20 centimetres high, they are white and resemble little trees with lots of tiny branches. They are sea pens, relatives of sea anemones and corals. They come out at night to filter feed. If they are gently stroked they sparkle with dozens of pinpricks of light that shoot from base to tip and back again. They look rather like miniature marine Christmas trees. Why they should do this is a bit of a mystery.

Sandy sea beds are also home to creatures with an uncanny resemblance to alien spacecraft: fire urchins. They cruise across the seafloor and, in the beam of a torch, glow a rich orangy-red with fiery flashes of yellow and blue. The deep red glow comes from the centre of their body and the flashes from hundreds of venom-tipped spines. They do not produce their own light, but reflect the torchlight in this intriguing way. Why such nocturnal creatures should be so brightly coloured is still unknown.

Some of the most dangerous hunters of the night do not need light at all. For their size, cone shells, which are a type of marine snail, are some of the deadliest animals to be found around the reef. Buried in the sand, they are as dangerous as hidden mines. Although only a few centimetres long, they have occasionally inflicted fatal wounds on humans. A cone shell's normal prey is other molluscs or small fish. It detects their presence with a powerful sense of smell. As they approach it brings its lethal poison harpoon into play. With lightning speed, not something usually associated with snails, it fires the harpoon. Death for the unsuspecting prey is almost instantaneous. It needs to be because a carnivorous snail is too slow to be able to chase a wounded and fleeing fish or other potential meal.

At night the nature of the reef itself changes. Most corals do their feeding in the dark. As shadows creep into cracks and crevices on the reef it is in these places that the coral polyps first unfurl their tentacles. Each tiny polyp is an individual animal and just as voracious a hunter as any carnivorous fish. Their handicap is that they cannot move. Instead they must exploit the behaviour of their prey to bring them within eating distance. Just after sunset many of the minuscule and microscopic animals that have spent the day lower in the water column, or even hidden in the reef, rise to the surface. These small crustaceans, molluscs and the many other species that make up the zooplankton, rise towards a million waiting mouths. As the currents sweep the soupy mix of tiny creatures over the reef the coral polyps ensnare individual animals with their sticky and stinging tentacles.

There are zooplankton around during the day too, just not quite as many. But corals have other reasons for remaining hidden within their hard calcareous skeletons when the sun is up. For one, they would stand a much greater chance of being nibbled and eaten by fish who would find it easy to spot the waving tentacles in the bright light of day. But open tentacles at this time might also shade the symbiotic algae living within the coral and inhibit their photosynthesis. That would reduce the quantity of nutrients the zooxanthellae were able to pass on to the coral. The relationship is evidently not a simple one. The partnership of plant and carnivorous animal allows them to exploit their environment for food and sustenance almost twenty-four hours a day.

Most tropical seas are clear and blue. There are very few nutrients to cloud the waters. Because of this they are generally poor in marine life. It is only in special places such as coral reefs that life can thrive in abundance. The animals and plants combine to overcome the original lack of nutrients. The zooxanthellae get the system going by harnessing sunlight. As they and the corals grow together to build the reef it in turn provides a substrate which other plants can colonise. They then harness yet more of the sun's energy in photosynthesis. It is, in fact, these other plants, which cover the reef in a microscopic film, that provide most of the food to support the large populations of animals that live around the coral.

The whole system is finely balanced to work in crystal clear waters. But New Guinea has an abundance of three linked factors that can change those conditions literally overnight: mountains, rivers and rain. The mountains create the rain, which then washes away the surface of the mountains, which travels in huge rivers to be dumped into the sea. And when large quantities of mountain end up in the sea it does not stay crystal clear for long.

New Guinea has two rivers, the Sepik and the Fly, that rank among the world's greatest in terms of the amount of water and sediment they discharge. It has been estimated that the Fly carries in suspension about 400 million tonnes of rock and soil each year. The Sepik flows out into the ocean with such volume and force that 60 kilometres from its mouth villagers on the island of Manam can collect fresh water from the sea.

In places the flow from small rivers actually fertilises reefs with nutrients. The reef at Madang, for example, may on one day be clear and then after a night of rain be almost obscured by waters murky with dissolved sediment. This runoff from the land is annoy-ing for divers but, on balance, probably enriches the coral. In locations where the sediment is too thick it smothers any coral trying to grow, and in cloudy waters the zooxanthellae cannot photosynthesise properly.

Mangroves thrive in really murky waters. These trees are really terrestrial plants that happen to be able to live with their roots in salt water. They still require their leaves to be above the surface and so can only survive in the shallows. Further out, and where the water is too cloudy for coral to start growing, seagrass thrives. It cannot cope with being smothered but it can put to good use a certain amount of suspended sediment. Unlike almost all other truly marine plants, including seaweeds, it is not a type of algae but a proper flowering plant that at some stage in its evolutionary history has taken to salt water.

Vast beds of seagrass grow around the coasts of New Guinea. The Torres Strait, between northern Queensland and southern Papua New Guinea, is one of the largest and most productive areas of seagrass in the world. The short blades sway in the current like a meadow of long grass blowing back and forth in the breeze. At first sight they often look as barren as a well-manicured lawn, but only because the life they support is hidden down amongst the stems in the first few centimetres of water above the sea floor.

The productivity of these meadows is phenomenal. In the middle of the day, with every blade of grass harnessing the energy of the sun at maximum rate, bubbles of oxygen stream to the surface, a by-product of the photosynthesis that is turning sunlight and water into yet more grass. Because these meadows trap a great deal of suspended sediment they are also well fertilised with all the nutrients essential for growth.

The result is a habitat as rich as the reef itself, and vital for the animals of the reef too. Many of the fish that in later life will swim and feed around the coral spend their early days in the seagrass. It's an ideal nursery. The pickings are rich and the predators fewer here. Attached to almost every piece of grass are tiny bryozoa, fan worms, sea anemones and other small invertebrate animals. Around the roots crawl brightly coloured shrimps, crabs and lobsters. In between the blades swim trigger fish, plucking at the tiny creatures anchored to the grass. Puffer fish glide about, using sensitive fins to manoeuvre their box-like bodies through the maze. Most appealing of all are the highly camouflaged sea-horses. They wait patiently, grasping a stem with their prehensile tails. When an unsuspecting shrimp passes by they shoot out and suck it in with their vacuum of a snout.

Just as on the great savannas of Africa or the prairies of North America these grasslands have their herds of large grazing herbivores: dugongs, or sea cows as they are sometimes known. They are slow and placid animals, may grow to nearly a tonne in weight, and can live for up to fifty years. Dugongs, or their close relatives, the manatees, were the animals on which the early legends of mermaids were based.

Sometimes shy, but on other occasions remarkably curious, their relationship with man has not been a happy one. They have been hunted for their meat, oil and tusks so that in many places they have been eliminated or much reduced. Today there are very few places left where large herds remain. Their great size, a thick skin and blood that clots very fast seem to be their only means of defence. Against men with spears in paddle-powered canoes they just about managed to hold their own. Today the canoes are powered by fast outboard motors. The dugongs do not stand a chance.

All in all, dugongs are not nearly as finely adapted to an aquatic existence as seals, dolphins, whales and other marine mammals. They can stay submerged for only a maximum of two to three minutes before they have to surface to breathe, and that's if they are resting. When actively feeding they can hold their breath for only about a minute, rather less than a well-trained diver! This limits the depth at which they can feed efficiently to about 5 metres, but that is not too much of a handicap as seagrass does not grow much deeper.

Although they graze on the leaves, they much prefer the succulent roots which they grub up with their snout, rather like a pig. The end of their snout is fashioned into a horseshoe-shaped plate covered in hairs. Some are delicate and may be sense organs, but others are stout and used as rakes for feeding. Whether eating roots or leaves the dugong sticks its head down into the grass and flares out the edge of this disc. The bristles hook onto pieces of plant which are then passed back towards the mouth, as if on a conveyor belt, by waves of muscular contraction rolling over the disc. Dugongs do not have a proper set of teeth, only small peg-like molars at the back of their mouths, and in males two short tusks. Instead they use rough, horny pads on their upper and lower palate to chew their food.

Seagrass is eaten by very few other animals because it is tough and full of indigestible cellulose. Dugongs only manage on this diet by eating vast quantities of the stuff and processing it not only in their mouths but also in their extremely long intestines. A large dugong may have to consume up to 40 kilogrammes a day to be able to extract sufficient nutrients to survive. As they feed they leave long and easily visible trails in the fields of seagrass.

Local people on the south coast of Papua New Guinea, near the town of Daru, use these trails when hunting for them. But to find the tracks in the first place they have to know in which part of the sea to look. Dugongs move predictably with the moon and tides. At full moon they will be in one place, at new moon in another, and the local people know this. The extent of the hunters' knowledge is so great they can even sex them underwater by their breathing rate. Males apparently breathe much faster than females and cough like old men when they surface.

With a limited ability to dive, slow speed and a lack of stamina, dugongs, despite their large size, are confined to shallow coastal waters. Other giants that cruise the same seas are not so restricted in their range, and one of the best places to observe them is at the diving resort of Walindi on the island of New Britain. Here the mountains plunge steeply into the sea, and close inshore the water is clear and deep. It is rated as one of the best diving sites in the world. Great pillars of rock rise through the depths and support magnificent coral reefs. But as well as superb coral there are much larger creatures here. In fact the largest fish in the world, the whale shark, sometimes cruises by, as well as other sharks, dolphins and whales. The whale shark itself, up to 15 metres long, is a true ocean wanderer. It is here in search of the same food that coral polyps feed on – zooplankton. With mouth agape it filters them from the water.

The other carnivores are in search of much larger prey. It is not too uncommon to meet a pod of killer whales. Although their food tends to come in bite-sized lumps about the size of a human being, they do not seem to be aggressive towards mankind. Many divers have swum with them, even witnessed them feeding, without any hint of danger. In colder waters seals and sealions are some of their favourite food, but in these warm tropical seas they have been seen eating manta rays, large sunfish and sharks.

Great shoals of silvery barracuda are extremely common. They hunt in large numbers, sometimes in groups several hundred strong, cruising effortlessly in mid-water. Although they have a fearsome reputation, they rarely, if ever, attack people. Occasionally they will form into huge circles and swim round and round for several minutes before suddenly taking off in a certain direction. It's a spectacular sight, especially from below when the shoal is dramatically silhouetted against the surface.

Food is not the only reason that wanderers visit the waters of New Guinea. In among the myriad tiny islands of Milne Bay province at the far eastern end of the island is a location, only discovered in 1987, to which large numbers of sharks come at certain times of the year. These are hammerheads, sinister-looking fish with snouts flattened out into a broad wing. They are quite common around the rest of New Guinea where they hunt for food along the sheer walls on the ocean side of reefs. But here the sharks are more interested in each other than in eating: they have come to mate. Such breeding aggregations of hammerheads have been sighted in other locations around the world, such as the sea of Cortez in Mexico, and so it is perhaps not surprising that they are found here too. But no one knows why they should choose to visit this particular spot rather than any other around New Guinea.

There is no such mystery surrounding the preferred breeding location for the final group of large animals to cruise these waters – the turtles. Their main requirement is a quiet sandy beach in which they can lay their eggs. With a great variety of good beaches and its central position on the ocean highways New Guinea is a mecca for turtles. Of the seven species found worldwide, six swim in the waters around the island.

The largest of them all is the leatherback which can weigh over half a tonne. New Guinea has the largest and most important leatherback nesting beaches in the southern hemisphere. They are on the Vogelkop Peninsula in Irian Jaya. In one year over 13 000 clutches of eggs can be laid here. As each female may have up to five clutches in a season this means that about 2500 turtles come ashore during the nesting period between April and October. In some years the numbers are much lower because leatherback females nest only in alternate years, or even only once every three years. In the intervening period little is known about the habits of these great ocean wanderers. They certainly travel far and wide in search of their preferred prey, jellyfish. But after swimming continuously for several years and covering thousands of kilometres of sea they return unerringly to the beaches on which they were born.

Not all the marine animals that live around the shores of New Guinea arrive quite so deliberately. But because of its central location, between several different seas, the island's coastline receives the flow from a great variety of currents, and these bring with them a selection of underwater life as diverse as that found anywhere else on earth. Most of this life is, in many ways, quite similar to that found elsewhere in the Indian and Pacific Oceans because the water that links the whole region acts as a highway for marine creatures.

The water has had an equally profound but completely different effect on land-living animals. For them it has acted as a barrier, isolating the island's wildlife, allowing few new species to arrive and containing those that already live there. Thus, the fauna and flora of the forests and mountains of the interior have evolved in their own unique and fascinating ways, as the following chapters reveal.

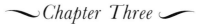

Chapter Three

KANGAROOS
IN THE TREES

*I*n most rainforests there is never any need for an alarm clock in the mornings. The piercing calls of some monkey or ape greeting the sunrise are usually loud enough to stir even the deepest sleepers. In Africa it might be the rasping voice of a colobus monkey, in South America the throaty roar of a howler, or in Asia the melodious song of a gibbon. In the rainforests of New Guinea the dawn is strangely quiet.

The island has some of the greatest undisturbed tracts of tropical rainforest in the world and all are ideal habitat for primates. But none has ever found their way here. Instead New Guinea has evolved its own unique range of tree-living marsupial mammals: striped and feather-tailed possums, ringtails, cuscuses and tree kangaroos. Few of these have loud calls and if you were lucky enough to hear one it would be much more likely to be in the middle of the night because most are entirely nocturnal. At dawn they return to a comfortable fork or tree hole, or settle down in a nest of leaves high in the canopy.

Primates and many other groups of non-marsupial mammals, do not live here for one simple reason. Australia and New Guinea have not been connected to any other continent for over forty million years. In their island isolation the early mammals of Australia evolved in a unique way, protected from the invasion of competitors by the surrounding sea. Many millions of years later, when the mountains of New Guinea were finally pushed up and forest clothed their flanks, it was from this stock of Australian animals that the forest dwellers of New Guinea developed.

The most famous of all Australia's mammals are undoubtedly the kangaroos, but for clambering in a rainforest canopy it is hard to imagine a less suitable design. Their massive hind legs have evolved for hopping and can only move together. The left and the right cannot swing forwards and backwards independently, as required for climbing. Their arms are small and their hands poor at gripping, and their huge tail is designed for balancing at high speed on the ground rather than for support in the trees. Yet, with a rich new source of food and living space waiting to be exploited, and with no real competitors to keep them out of the trees, kangaroos that could climb up into the canopy did eventually evolve. Today the island has several different species of tree kangaroo, some in lowland forest, others higher up and some even in the cold stunted woodlands near the mountain tops.

To help them adapt to this new arboreal life their bodies have changed considerably. Their forearms have grown stouter and more muscular to give them a stronger grip. Their hind legs have become smaller and can be moved independently, and their feet have become broader with non-slip soles. But all this does not add up to a very convincing monkey substitute. Most still seem terribly ungainly in the trees and, with their broad kangaroo mouth and tiny eyes, often look genuinely perplexed about which way to go or what to do next. The youngsters are least confident of all, often standing at the end of a branch turning this way and that, deciding whether to attempt it head or feet first. They usually go for the safer option, especially when climbing down, of hugging the branch tightly with their forepaws and gently slithering backwards. On horizontal boughs, and when in more confident mood, tree kanga-roos hop along with their tail held out behind just like their ground-living ancestors. Although they do not regularly leap great distances, they will jump from tree to tree if disturbed and have even been known, in moments of danger, to fling themselves to the ground from a height of over 15 metres.

The reason they are up in the trees at all is the potential harvest of great quantities of leaves and fruit. Rainforest leaves may look green and succulent compared with the grasses and shrubs that ordinary kangaroos feed on but they are tough and just as difficult to digest. To cope with this problematic diet tree kangaroos have large, distended stomachs giving them a pot-bellied appearance just like leaf-eating monkeys. This allows them to ingest a lot of food at once and to leave it in their gut for a long period of time to ferment. Bacteria in the stomach break down the tough cellulose in the leaves and allow the kangaroos to extract the maximum amount of nutrients from their meals.

But despite all their adaptations, it is quite obvious that most of these kangaroos have not yet entirely mastered tree life. They often slide back down to the ground to hop about, snuffling for young shoots, fallen fruit or other tasty morsels on the forest floor. Other New Guinea mammals perhaps come closer to filling the role of the missing primates.

Looking up into the canopy you would have to be very lucky indeed to glimpse the round, furry face and large red-rimmed eyes of the common spotted cuscus. Although one of the most spectacular and interesting of the island's animals, it is secretive and mainly nocturnal. In stature it resembles a rather cuddly little bear with a long tail, but in fact it is related to possums. Highly adapted to a life in the trees, it spends almost all its time aloft, feeding on leaves, fruit and flowers very much like a monkey, if somewhat slower.

Primates have a good grip because they can press their thumb against the rest of their fingers. The toes on a cuscus's front feet can also be positioned in a similar way to create a pincer-like grasp. If this is not sufficient to lock the animal to a branch it also has a long prehensile tail that acts as an additional mobile limb. The final two-thirds of the tail is naked and contains rough bumps on its inner surface. It's surprisingly similar to the tail of a howler monkey which also has a naked and bumpy inner surface to increase friction on the wood being grasped.

Common spotted cuscuses also resemble certain primates in a more curious way. Some forest-living monkeys have conspicuous patches of colour on parts of their anatomy, and these marsupials also have bold colour patterns, often over much of their body. Some are orange-brown with splashes of white, others are grey and white, while on a few the patches merge entirely to create a startling all-white coat. Males are larger than females and tend to be more conspicuously marked. Although there is a great deal of geographical and individual variation, they are often white with several darker spots: females tend to have white only on their head and neck. The lower parts of the female's body are usually brown or even black.

These bright and varied colour schemes certainly cannot be for camouflage, and probably do not need to be because there are no large predators active after dark when the cuscuses are moving around. Because the patterns are different in males and females they most likely perform a social function. Many forest monkeys have distinctive colours on parts of their bodies to identify themselves to other troop members in the gloom of the forest interior. In other species bright male colours send sexual signals to potential rivals and mates. Little is known about the spotted cuscus's social organisation but it does not seem to be a very gregarious animal with a regular need to signal to other members of its species. On the other hand, a nocturnal animal with bright white in its coat certainly seems to be drawing attention to itself. The answer, as with so much of New Guinea's natural history, is that there are almost certainly aspects of cuscus behaviour yet to be discovered. It could be far more social than anyone has yet guessed.

The tree kangaroos and cuscuses are relatively large and slow-moving animals, but there are also many small and agile marsupial mammals scurrying up and down the trunks and leaping around among the finer branches. They too are unique to these forests, yet have evolved in ways that are remarkably similar to the lemurs, bushbabies and marmosets of other continents. No matter what the individual species of trees, the rainforests of New Guinea are ecologically very similar to those elsewhere in the world and provide the same sorts of food on which animals can specialise, the most plentiful, of course, being leaves.

The New Guinea ringtail possums eat an almost exclusive diet of leaves and, as with tree kangaroos and leaf-eating monkeys, have developed large intestines to cope. They have a special side pocket in their hind gut called the caecum. It harbours microbes that aid digestion by breaking down tough plant matter. But being relatively small animals to start with, there is a limit to the size the gut can grow. The solution has been to evolve a powerful battery of grinding teeth to reduce their highly fibrous diet to a manageable paste before swallowing it.

The sugar glider, on the other hand, takes meals that need no chewing at all. It feeds on sap and gum, often biting into the bark of a tree to encourage the liquids to flow and then lapping them up with its tongue. Suitable feeding sites may be several hundred metres apart but, as its name suggests, the sugar glider has an unusual means of travel. Just like the flying squirrels of Asia, it has a flap of skin stretched between its legs on either side of its body. It launches itself into the air from a high branch and glides from tree to tree over distances of up to 50 metres at a time. By changing the curvature of each wing flap the glider is able to steer itself accurately for a perfect landing each time.

Because of their ability to travel from tree to tree without descending to the ground, sugar gliders are able to live in more open woodland than many of the other more strictly forest-dwelling mammals. Paperbark and eucalyptus are among their favourite trees. Feeding sites where the right sort of sap or gum flow freely are highly prized and are ferociously defended by chasing and biting intruders. Flowering trees, on the other hand, can provide a feast for many animals. I have often seen them licking the nectar from eucalyptus blossoms.

Sugar gliders are fascinating little animals with well-developed social behaviour. They tend to nest in tree holes, and several adults and their young may share a single hole. The dominant male has special scent glands on various parts of his body and he marks all other members of the colony with a distinctive odour. Identification is by smell, and in this way relatives can be distinguished from strangers. They also groom each other and in the process spread odours from their salivary glands from one animal to the next. These activities also help them maintain strong social bonds.

Insects and other small invertebrates abound in the rainforest and gliders catch them when they can, but there is one small marsupial that has evolved especially to hunt insects hidden beneath bark. The striped possum is a startling creature with black and white stripes stretching the length of its body, giving it a skunk-like

40 ABOVE: *The southern savannas of New Guinea were connected by land to northern Australia until about 6000 years ago and today both areas still share similar climates. As a result, both have many species of animal in common, such as this agile wallaby.*

42 ABOVE: *The short-beaked echidna is an egg-laying mammal related to the duck-billed platypus. It lives in both Australia and New Guinea. The spines provide protection. When threatened, the animal can roll itself into a ball, just like a hedgehog.*

43 BELOW: Monitor lizards use their forked tongues in the same way as snakes – to detect the faintest smell of prey or carrion.

44 RIGHT: Huge flocks of magpie geese descend on the Bensbach Plains each year. They are here for the rich grazing, created as water levels drop and aquatic plants become exposed.

45 PREVIOUS PAGE: *Australian pelicans often migrate north to the swamps of New Guinea, especially if there is a drought in Australia.*

46 ABOVE: *A pied heron stalks its prey in a shallow pool on the Bensbach Plains.*

47 RIGHT: *The Asmat people inhabit a vast area of swampland in Irian Jaya. Until recently, they were enthusiastic headhunters, using their war canoes to launch raids against neighbouring villages.*

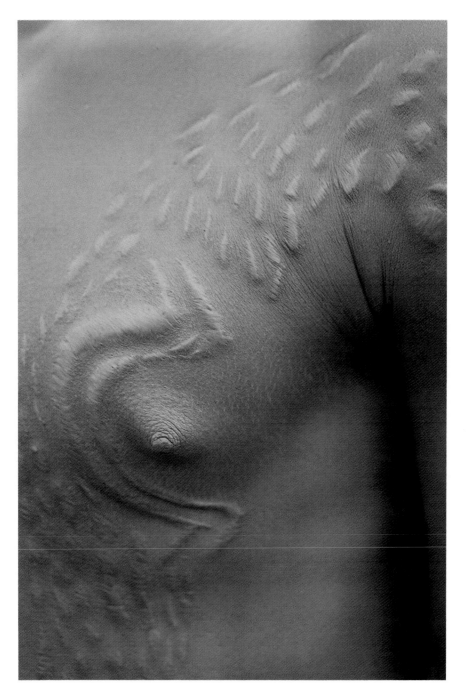

48 LEFT: *Like many tribal groups in New Guinea, the Asmat people hunt birds of paradise for their feathers, which they use for personal adornment.*

49 ABOVE: *Many young men of the Sepik Region have their skin cut in ritual patterns which resemble the slashes and tooth bites which might be made by an attacking crocodile.*

*50 LEFT: Rivers are just about the
only highways through the dense
swamplands that cover vast areas of
lowland New Guinea.*

*51 ABOVE: Saltwater crocodiles
have found their way hundreds of
kilometres upstream and now
inhabit stretches of river far away
from the sea.*

52 **BELOW:** *The comb-crested jacana lives all its life on floating vegetation, even nesting here.*

53 **RIGHT:** *In shallow water, at the edge of the Blackwater River, water lilies provide a splash of colour.*

54 **ABOVE:** *Along the Karawari
River, the banks are clothed in dense
forest from which hang bright
blooms of D'Albertis creeper, better
known as 'flame of the forest'.*

55 Salvadori's monitor (ABOVE) is found only in New Guinea and is the longest lizard in the world.

appearance. These markings are a warning to other animals to keep away because, like the skunk, it produces a pungent odour that is clinging and noxious. There are four species, all reasonably similar in appearance.

A small animal, highly agile and erratic in its movements, it darts here and there, leaping from tree to tree, ranging through the lower canopy and across the forest floor in search of tree trunks, limbs and rotten logs that might conceal succulent woodboring grubs. It has a curious splayed nose to sniff out its prey, and as it moves over the bark it taps the surface gently, listening for the tell-tale hollow ring of an insect's burrow.

One species of striped possum, called the long-fingered triok, has evolved similar anatomical specialisations for catching prey to the unusual Madagascan lemur, the aye aye. Like the aye aye, it sports long incisor teeth for prising open bark and an elongated fourth finger to winkle out grubs or other insects. The possum's presence is often given away by the slurping and sucking noises it makes as it devours its juicy meal.

Feathertail possums also eat insects but in a rather different way. They are called feathertails because their long tails have two rows of hairs sticking out on either side, giving them a feathery appearance. These animals use their tails to help them balance and hang on. They are tiny, very active, and agile as their family name, Acrobatidae, suggests. They leap on prey such as grasshoppers, bush crickets and cicadas and then bite through their heads to immobilise them. By removing the head, or another part of the external skeleton of the victim, they create a hole through which they can insert their tongue. This is long and pointed, and contains lots of tiny backward-pointing papillae on its surface. These help the possum to hook lumps of insect flesh and pull them out through the hole.

Primates were not the only group of mammals to fail to reach New Guinea. No carnivores arrived either, except for dogs introduced by man. But in this case the marsupials do not seem to have been very successful in evolving species to take on this role. Among the fifty or so different marsupials on the island it is quite remarkable that there are no large predators. In fact the largest flesh-eating animals in New Guinea are birds and reptiles.

A range of small, predatory marsupials have evolved, however.

They are quite unlike the cats, weasels or other smaller carnivores of the rest of the non-Australian world, and have strange names to match. Names like planigale, antechinus, dunnart and dasyure. Most are secretive, many are rare, and almost all are very poorly known. In most cases their hunting behaviour has never been observed so it is not known exactly what they eat, but a good idea of the type of prey they could tackle can be inferred from studying their appearance. Most are more like mice than cats in shape, with pointed snouts and long thin tails, but their teeth give them away as true predators. Most probably hunt invertebrates although they will tackle mice, frogs, small lizards and birds. Some of the smaller species also eat fruit and flowers from time to time.

The only real exceptions to this mouse-like appearance are the quolls, sometimes called marsupial 'cats'. There are two species and both are immediately recognisable by their brown coats covered in bright white spots. With a rounded head, large bright eyes and a glistening pink nose they are very attractive animals. They are also fierce predators and will attack prey larger than themselves.

The New Guinea quoll inhabits rainforest and is relatively well known. The bronze quoll is the largest marsupial predator on the island, but, remarkably, was not discovered by science until 1979. Since then only a handful of specimens have been collected. These have all come from a small area of savanna woodland near Moore-head, in the far south of New Guinea.

Also scampering around on the forest floor are an assortment of marsupial herbivores. The spotted cuscus, which spends most of its time in the trees, has a relative that burrows underground. The ground cuscus is a relatively common animal but not often seen because it remains hidden away during the day, resting in shallow tunnels beneath tree roots, or even in caves. It seems to favour a diet of fruit but occasionally it has been seen catching small animals, such as grasshoppers, rats, lizards, and even toads.

In contrast to the bright markings of its spotted relative, the ground cuscus is covered with dull grey fur. This species seems to inhabit a world where social signals are transmitted not by a colour-ful coat but by smells. Ground cuscuses mark their home ranges with urine and with a pungent substance exuded from special scent glands. If animals meet they can be quite violent, fighting with their claws and teeth, and sometimes seriously injuring each other.

Also down on the ground are several species of kangaroo; not all have taken to the trees. Apart from the agile wallaby, which inhabits the savannas in the south of the island, all the other seven species of terrestrial kangaroo are forest dwellers. Unlike the large and strongly built kangaroos of the open plains of Australia, these are dainty little animals and often shy. They have been hunted extensively wherever they live near human settlements, and this may explain why they tend to be far more active at night than during the daytime.

Even more inconspicuous, because of their small size, are the bandicoots. In appearance they are a little like rats, with pointed snouts and long thin tails. But their habits are far more attractive than those of the average rat. They bound around with a characteristic gait, using their noses to search out a tasty insect or a piece of ripe fruit. Their ears are quite large and bare. They seem to be able to move them like miniature radar dishes to locate the origin of a particular sound.

Like all female marsupials, bandicoot mothers have a pouch in which to keep their developing young. But because they are always rushing around with their belly close to the ground, a pouch which opens forward like that of a kangaroo could be rather awkward: there would always be the chance of dirt or a stick or other obstruction getting caught in the opening. The solution is to have a pouch with the opening facing backwards. To get inside the youngsters have to race behind their mother and dive in between her back legs. The females are very productive breeding machines compared with other marsupials. The young develop swiftly in the pouch and the mother has litter after litter in quick succession.

The strangest of all the mammals that snuffle around on the forest floor is not a marsupial but a rather more unusual type of animal related to the duck-billed platypus. It has spines, a very long thin snout and a barbed tongue. But these are not its most unusual attributes. It is a mammal that lays eggs, which is almost, but not quite, a total contradiction. For this reason the spiny anteater or echidna is placed together with the duck-billed platypus in a group called the monotremes. There are two species in New Guinea, a smaller one that also lives in Australia, and a rather larger one, weighing up to 10 kilogrammes, which is unique to New Guinea. It is appropriately named the giant spiny anteater, or the long-beaked echidna.

It has long spines all over the back and sides of its body which are often hidden by its dense brown fur, making some look positively cuddly. But picking one up is not recommended. Both spines and claws are sharp, and for its size it is a powerful animal. In spite of its name the giant spiny anteater does not eat ants very often. It prefers juicy earthworms which it is well adapted to catch. It has powerful claws for digging and a long slender snout for inserting down worm holes. Its snout is so narrow, however, that the echidna has to find the end of a worm before it can swallow it. Once either the head or tail has been located this specialised worm hunter extrudes a unique tongue with backward pointing spines at its tip. The worm is impaled on the spines and then winched into the echidna's mouth. It is a charming and highly inquisitive animal, but unfortunately it has been heavily hunted for its meat and is now rare over most of its range.

All these marsupials and monotremes have evolved in parallel with, but in isolation from, the rest of the non-Australian world because of the surrounding ocean. But the water has not been an obstacle for fruit bats.

Bats are the only mammals capable of sustained flight rather than the brief airborne journeys of animals like the sugar glider. Fruit bats are the largest bats of all, some having a wingspan of over $1\frac{1}{2}$ metres, and can fly the furthest. The stretch of sea separating South East Asia and New Guinea has always been at least a hundred kilometres wide but has proved a relatively easy barrier for them to cross. With the huge variety of habitats available, and also perhaps because of the lack of fruit-eating primates, these bats have undergone an explosive evolution on the mainland of New Guinea and on many of the smaller surrounding islands too. Today there are over fifty different species living in this area, about a third of the earth's total: New Guinea is the fruit bat capital of the world. Many species may actually have evolved in New Guinea first and then spread elsewhere in the tropics, rather than the other way around.

The largest fruit bats of all belong to the genus *Pteropus* and are commonly called flying foxes. Right in the town of Madang on the north coast of Papua New Guinea there are several large roosts of spectacled flying foxes. Most are in tall casuarina trees and the largest roost of all is in a group of these standing right outside the main police station. The sight, sound and smell of tens of thousands of flying foxes is almost overwhelming. Even during the day they hardly sleep and the roost is alive with moving bodies and constant squealing and squawking.

They tend to be especially active in the first hour or two in the morning, just after their nightly forays. In the right season males persistently thrust themselves on females. Mating seems to be pretty aggressive, with the pair apparently attacking each other before they finally embrace. They spin round and round and swing from side to side while copulating. It is amazing that they do not loose their grip and fall off. As the sun gains strength the colony quietens down a little and most of the bats start to flap their great black wings back and forth in the breeze. This helps keep their bodies cool.

When the bats are at their most energetic in the early morning and late afternoon they sometimes break off finer branches, causing those hanging from them to rise in noisy flight to find a more secure resting spot. Many of the bats have wings covered in scars and tears. These could be either from crash landings or, more likely, the result of fighting. As the day wears on and evening approaches more and more bats take to the air, but they often travel only a short distance before resting in another nearby tree.

It is just before dusk that the most impressive spectacle begins. Against the deep red glow of the dying sun thousands upon thousands of dark silhouettes take to the air. Their flight is slow and deliberate. Groups head off in all directions in search of fruiting trees. At times the sky is completely covered with bats. Wave after wave pass overhead, reminiscent of squadrons of wartime bombers.

As the light finally fades some bats reach open water between the fingers of mangrove that grow out into the Madang Lagoon. Their wing beats ease and they glide gently down to the surface of the sea. Just as a crash landing appears inevitable they flap, splash across the waves, and once more take to the air. A single bat often repeats this odd manoeuvre several times before finally flying off to feed. They do not seem to be drinking, although some people have claimed that this is what they are doing. The true function of this strange behaviour simply is not known. Could the salt condition their fur perhaps?

A few biologists have suggested they may be trying to pluck fruit from the water. In 1954 a colonial administrator in Dutch New Guinea observed several large flying foxes trying to do just that. Some not only failed to grab the fruit but also crashed into the sea. Unable to flap their way up from the water surface, they lay there with wings outstretched until the current had propelled them to the shore. It was dawn, and in the early morning light they scrambled through the small waves at the water's edge and dragged themselves up the beach until they found some saplings into which they could climb. Once they had gained a height of a few metres they launched themselves back into the air. There is no report of whether they continued to try and retrieve the fruit or simply headed off for their roost.

The spectacled flying foxes are so named because of a rim of light coloured fur around their eyes. In fact they have excellent vision, especially at night, and a keen sense of smell with which to search out ripening fruit. All fruit bats consume an enormous quantity of food and a flying fox may eat its weight in fruit every night. They bite into their meal and then squeeze out the juice between their teeth, their tongue and the roughened roof of their mouth. Swallowing the juice and any small seeds, they then spit out the fibrous pulp. Such a liquid diet passes through their gut rather quickly, in fact sometimes in ten to fifteen minutes flat, so it's best not to stand underneath a group of them feeding!

Because fruit bats consume seeds and then pass them out before they have had time to be digested, they are extremely important for dispersing seeds in the New Guinea forests. Many species also feed on nectar and, from the coasts right up into the highlands, bats are among the major pollinators of forest trees. By visiting bloom after bloom they pick up pollen in their fur and then transfer it to the next flower. In fact some trees, such as the paperbark, flower solely at night to ensure that they attract only bats. The blossom bats are some of the most important pollinators of all because they specialise in nectar feeding. They have a pointed muzzle and a long, brush-like tongue to probe right down to the flowers' nectaries. If the petals are just too long, as they are in a few trumpet-shaped flowers, blossom bats can nip a hole in the base and then delicately insert their tongue. They are the best hoverers of all fruit bats and flit from bloom to bloom as easily as hummingbirds. They also use their agility in flight to beat off interlopers when they try to muscle in on a particularly prolific and valuable blossom.

New Guinea has a great variety of caves and at first this might seem like a bonus for the bats. But unlike their smaller cousins, the insect eaters, most fruit bats cannot echolocate. They have excellent vision but in pitch blackness even the best eyesight is useless. So very few of them can roost in caves. One exception is the *Rousettus* fruit bat which does have a rather simple echolocating ability. Another species which uses parts of caves where there is some light is the bare-backed fruit bat. It has such a strange name because its wing membranes, which are devoid of fur, extend right over its back and meet in the midline just over the spine. These unusual wings give the bats increased manoeuvrability, a definite advantage in the confined passages of a cave.

Near Madang is a large roost of these bats. They hang in their hundreds of thousands on the sheer limestone wall of a sink-hole over 30 metres deep. They flit in and out of the cavern at the base of the cliff. It's quite a feat of flying for such large bats to descend into the limestone hole, especially if several hundred other bats are in the air at the same time. But the bare-backed fruit bats display their aerial agility in a spectacular way.

They come spiralling down out of the sky in tight circles, the wind audibly whistling in their wings. As they fall they tip their wings from side to side, spilling air to hasten their descent into the gaping hole. They twist, turn, and dive to avoid other bats in their way. The limestone wall for which the fliers are aiming is black with a heaving mass of bats. There often does not seem to be any available space, but each incoming bat selects a certain spot and heads for it. At the very last moment it spreads its wings to brake and performs a sharp turn to alight upside down, grabbing at any tiny roughness on the rock. The neighbouring bats move aside a little and a living ripple spreads across the wall as thousands of nearby bodies adjust their positions.

Because fruit bats roost in huge numbers many species have

developed a considerable variety of social behaviours. Large males defend territories, usually a metre or two of branch, and fight off rivals during the mating season. They display and groom as a preliminary to mating. When the babies are born they cling to their mothers for the first few weeks of their lives. They are born with well-developed claws and backwardly curving milk teeth, both of which help them maintain a strong grip on their mother's body. But when they become too heavy, and before they can fly themselves, groups of youngsters are left back at the roost while the adults fly away to feed.

With so many kinds of fruit bat New Guinea has several unusual species. One that is particularly bizarre in appearance is the tube-nosed bat, so called because of its strange snorkel-like nostrils. It roosts alone. Its wings are splashed with polka dots of yellow, and during the day it wraps these wings around its body. Hanging still and silent, it can be almost completely invisible among the sun-dappled foliage. There are several species of tube-nosed bat and one goes even further in its disguise. It has green wings. The colour may be natural or may, as in the South American sloth, be the result of algal growth.

Some species of tube-nosed bats do not seem to act like true fruit bats at all. Although they have the usual large eyes and foxy face, and certainly eat fruit at times, they also catch insects like their smaller echolocating relatives. This is very unusual behaviour for a fruit bat, but new species are regularly being described from New Guinea so there are likely to be even more surprises in store.

The smaller insectivorous bats are also quite numerous here but very few are unique to New Guinea. They belong to widespread groups with familiar names: pipistrelles, horseshoes, sheathtails and mastiffs. Some species are identical with those found many thousands of kilometres away in Asia and even further west. It seems that the insect eaters probably did not arrive on the island of New Guinea as early on as the fruit bats did and consequently have not yet evolved into such a variety of species.

Only one other group of mammals occurs naturally in New Guinea: rats and mice. New Guinea not only has lots of them; it has the largest in the world. The ancestors of today's rodents probably rafted over on floating vegetation. This must have been a very difficult route and only a relatively small number of animals survived the journey. As a result the rodent fauna of New Guinea is derived from just a few original ancestors. Some types have been here for millions of years and have now evolved into a great variety of forms; others arrived relatively recently. But together they now comprise one of the most diverse collections of rats and mice in the world. This probably results from two factors: New Guinea offers a great variety of places to live; and the rodents do not have to compete with other small mammals, like shrews or hedgehogs, which have simply never arrived on the island.

Most of the fifty or so species look and live like rats and mice anywhere in the world, but the giant rats are quite exceptional. There are several species weighing over a kilogramme. The largest of all weighs almost 2, and from nose to tail can be a metre long. Most of these giant rats live only in mountain forests where they are arboreal in habit, climbing along even slender branches.

The largest species has had a rather curious history of discovery. Although a specimen was first collected in 1945 by a patrol officer, it lay in a drawer in the Australian Museum, in Sydney, for forty years, unrecognised for what it was, not only a new species but probably the largest rat in the world. It was rediscovered in 1987 by one of the museum's mammal experts, Dr Tim Flannery. In the wild it remained undetected for so long because it lives only on some of the highest peaks on the island where it burrows in alpine grassland. Although very little is known about its biology, it does seem to have at least one very uncharacteristic feature, according to Dr Flannery. It has just one baby at a time.

Why this rodent should breed in such an apparently restrained manner remains a mystery, as do the habits of so many of New Guinea's poorly studied mammals. The isolation and rugged nature of the island have not only encouraged the evolution of many strange animals; they have also made it very difficult for zoologists to find and study them. Little is known about the behaviour and ecology of the vast majority of the island's mammals, and there are almost certainly several unknown species still awaiting discovery. Even at the very end of the twentieth century previously undescribed mammals continue to be found from time to time in the more remote and inaccessible parts of New Guinea.

Chapter Four

PARADISE ISLE

Wandering through the gloomy forest of Varirata National Park before sunrise is tricky. The park is only a forty minute drive from Port Moresby, the capital of Papua New Guinea, but it's a world apart. The land rises and falls in a series of steep hills and valleys. The earth underneath is wet, sticky and supremely slippery. At this time of day the tall trees let little light through to illuminate the way, and a fall into the mud is almost inevitable. But a journey to the centre of the forest so early in the morning is well worth the struggle. It is actually one of the easiest places on the whole island to observe the courtship display of a bird of paradise, and it is one of the most spectacular species of all, the raggiana bird of paradise.

Each morning just before dawn a group of males assemble at the top of one particular tree. Its crown is set slightly apart from the surrounding canopy and the birds themselves have opened up their arena further by defoliating most of the branches. As the sun's rays creep up over the hill this tree is one of the first in the valley to be bathed in the golden light of dawn.

The day I watched there were five males. At first they hopped from branch to branch gingerly, rather half-heartedly, I thought. Occasionally one might caw loudly. As the minutes passed the males slowly began to warm up. First one, then another, would display a splendid set of long, bright golden-red feathers from his flank. These are not feathers used in flight or to keep warm; they are far too frail and flimsy. They have only one function: to attract a mate.

Suddenly there is a cacophony of calling and all the males vigorously shake their plumes. There must be a female nearby. As she flies into the display area each male tries to win her attention. They throw out their wings, clap them together behind their backs, and send their brilliant golden feathers high above their heads. Each male tries to outdo the others. If the female mates at all it will only be with one, presumably the one she finds the most eye-catching. In an attempt to impress her the males hang upside down, their fabulous plumes cascading all around, living fountains of colour.

At last she seems to favour one and lingers by his perch. He remains hanging and thrusts the brightest part of his plumage up into the air and towards his potential mate. To show she is still interested she approaches and pecks at him. He leaps to her side and bobs up and down while beating his wings. His dancing becomes more frenzied. He sways from side to side as well as hopping up and down. At times he lunges and apparently strikes at the female with his bill. All the time he holds out his splendid plumes and shakes them in display. They catch the early morning light and seem to glow. Suddenly he's on top of her and two or three seconds later it's all over. The female flies off, and the successful male will have nothing further to do with her or the resulting eggs and young.

When birds of paradise were first described nothing was known about this or any other aspect of their interesting behaviour. The reason for this was that at first they were known only from their dead bodies. As early as the sixteenth century preserved skins had found their way back to Europe. The first arrived in Spain aboard one of the ships of Ferdinand Magellan. Europeans had never before seen birds of such exquisite and extravagant beauty. To add to the mystique surrounding these skins none seemed to have legs or feet. In fact these had been cut off by the original collectors, but people in Europe had another explanation. They believed that, with no feet or legs, these birds could not possibly land on earth and so must have come from a heavenly paradise in the sky. This idea, of course, tied in neatly with the bird's extraordinary feathers for which nobody at that time could imagine any purpose. Ever since then they have been known as the birds of paradise.

As New Guinea was explored in later centuries the truth slowly came to light, not only about these birds but also the many others that live here. Today well over 700 species of birds have been discovered on New Guinea and its offshore islands. The whole continent of Australia, almost ten times the size, has only about the same number.

But despite the great variety of birds that live here they are often difficult to see. The forest that clothes most of the island is tall and gloomy and many birds spend a great deal of their time in the canopy far above. Perhaps it is because of their dark forest habitat that many are so brightly coloured. Their plumage allows them to identify each other and helps them signal to other members of their species. From dainty little parrots that come in all colours of the rainbow, through large pigeons with splendid crowns, to the giant double-wattled cassowary with brilliant blue neck and scarlet throat pouch, many of New Guinea's birds are stunning. But none more so than those that so typify this place, the birds of paradise.

There are forty-three species in the world and thirty-eight of them live in New Guinea. Not all follow the style of the raggiana. Male astrapias, for example, have extended tails several times longer than their bodies. The king of Saxony bird of paradise, on the other hand, has very long feathers for display, but they shoot out from his head just behind the ears. The superb, in contrast, is a compact little bird that holds out a feathered shield of bright iridescent blue in front of its throat. Several species use not only their plumes to impress a potential mate but also brightly coloured linings inside their mouths.

A few species of birds of paradise are actually rather dull in colour and do not have showy courtship dances. Recent research in Papua New Guinea, especially by Bruce Beehler of the Smithsonian Institution, has revealed why some have evolved elaborate plumage and displays and others have not. In most species the female is very drab. It is only the males who go in for gaudy displays. Because females lay and look after the eggs they need to be well camouflaged from predators. If not, they and their clutch would become easy prey. But a male only needs to be camouflaged if he is going to help with incubation and rearing, and not all males do. To be able to leave the mother holding the baby, so to speak, the male must be sure that she is capable of rearing the young alone. Otherwise all his reproductive effort would be wasted.

The most crucial factor is the quality and quantity of food available. In the forests of New Guinea, just as in tropical rainforests worldwide, there are certain types of fruit with a high fat and protein content. These are very nutritious, but in most tropical forests squirrels and monkeys devour them. Here these fruits are there for the taking. The only snag is they tend to have a tough coat that is difficult to penetrate. But some birds of paradise have evolved beaks and claws that are strong enough to overcome this problem. With a supply of rich and nutritious fruit, supplemented by the odd insect, females of such species are easily able to raise and feed a brood by themselves. The males of the species tend to be the most colourful.

Although the females are drab, they are very desirable to a male because they will rear his young for him. Freed from this task himself, his main aim in life is to fertilise as many females as he can. This ensures that as many of his genes as possible are passed on to future generations. And how does he do this? Quite simply by making himself irresistible. Bold colours and vigorous dancing may also enable a male to intimidate his rivals into allowing him to use the best perch in a display area.

The females fall in with all this, because if they mate with the most attractive male they will tend to have attractive male offspring. These in turn will be successful breeders and will pass on their mother's genes to future generations. So the males compete with each other to be the most brilliant and eye-catching of the bunch. The whole evolutionary process is called sexual selection and was first recognised by Charles Darwin in the nineteenth century. Birds of paradise must surely be one of its most extravagant examples.

To be able to select a mate effectively a female needs to be able to compare them. In many species, like the raggiana, males perform together so this is not too difficult. This communal display is called a lek. Of course the males have their own reasons for coming together like this. In a dense forest it would be difficult to hunt out a specific female, much better to join other males and create such a racket that any female in the neighbourhood is bound to hear and come over to investigate. But in any one breeding season this ends in disappointment for most of them because females want to mate only with the best. Over 90 per cent of the copulations take place with just one male.

Not all birds of paradise behave like this. It's only possible to attract a lot of females from a large area to a communal display ground if the females themselves move about widely and are likely to come close to such a place. It may sometimes be better for the males to space themselves out a little. Each male may attract fewer females in the first place, but being alone he has a better chance of mating with them.

Many of the birds of paradise that adopt this sort of strategy seem to have display courts underneath the canopy or even on the forest floor. Down in the gloom they need feathers that are just as brilliant as those birds that dance in the tree-tops. Their entire bodies are sometimes brightly coloured and that makes these birds some of the most charming and exquisite jewels in the forest. The king, for example, is only 15 centimetres long but has back, wings and head that glow a deep crimson red. These are offset by a belly of pure white. Instead of a proper tail the male carries two delicate wires that end in a pair of iridescent emerald discs.

Each male has a territory in which he spends most of his time, surrounded by the territories of other males. Although they do not come together to display, they seem to prefer not to live too far apart. In each territory there is usually one or more special trees, often with dense vine-covered canopies, on which the bird displays. This he does on the tangled lianas and branches under the crown of the tree, but still quite high up.

The magnificent bird of paradise, on the other hand, displays right down on the forest floor. He is not much larger than the king and has orange wings, an iridescent green breast, and two long, curved tail feathers. The inside of the male's mouth is also coloured – bright yellowy-green. Part of the display involves flashing this at the female. Unlike the king, the magnificent prefers clear sky above his arena and chooses a spot with no canopy overhead. He then sets out to clear an area of the forest floor about 3 or 4 metres wide. This will be his dancing court. He picks up everything that can be moved from the surface of the ground and drags it aside. Leaves, twigs, dead insects, they must all go. To let in more light, and also to provide clean and convenient poles on which to display, he plucks the leaves from any saplings sprouting in the court.

He will keep this place for several years and goes to great lengths to keep it clean. Each day he inspects the court and removes any litter that has fallen in, or perhaps tugs at a particularly stubborn root that he has been trying to unearth for some time. In between cleaning up he preens his glossy plumage, practises a display or two, and calls to attract any nearby females.

The calls of birds of paradise are often as extraordinary as their appearance. The male magnificent can hiss, click, buzz and churr as well as producing many sounds that are far too difficult to describe. He also audibly rattles his wings. Some others make noises that sound more like electrical gadgets than bird-calls.

Although all these species look and sound very different from each other and behave in a variety of unique ways, they are all closely related. Studies of their genetic make-up show this clearly. But even more remarkable is that sometimes birds of different species do not recognise that they are different from one another.

It's hard to imagine a bright red male with golden plumes and a short beak being mistaken, say, for one with a dark body, bright blue breast, and a long curved beak. But that is just what happens from time to time. These birds, the raggiana and the magnificent riflebird, occasionally interbreed, as do many other mismatched pairs of birds of paradise. The resulting riot of colour in the male offspring can be quite extraordinary. One of the main functions of a distinct sexual display in any animal is to allow it to recognise others of its species. How ironic, then, that in the most ostentatious displayers of all this mechanism sometimes breaks down between, to our eyes at least, such obviously different birds.

Not all birds of paradise are brightly coloured. In fact there's one group, the manucodes, which is rather dull. Both male and female look similar and are largely black or dark purple. Unlike the more usual birds of paradise, male manucodes are monogamous. They establish a strong pair bond and may stay with the same partner for life. They also help in raising the young. Because of this they cannot mate with more than one female, so do not compete strongly with each other like other birds of paradise. Therefore, there is no advantage to being brightly coloured. In fact it would be a definite disadvantage while trying to sit quietly and unobserved, incubating eggs on a nest.

If the theory that male promiscuity depends on a nutritious diet is true, manucodes would be expected to eat less nourishing food. In many species the diet simply is not known. But in one, the trumpet manucode, it is. These birds feed largely on figs which are full of sugars but deficient in fats and proteins. They are not ideal for raising a hungry brood. They also grow on trees that are widely dispersed and come into fruit infrequently. In other words they need a lot of searching out. In such a situation it is certainly better to have two parents gathering food for the chicks. If they are to survive the male just does not have a choice about leaving, so he has to stay faithful and remain dull but dutiful.

There is another group of birds, closely related to the birds of paradise, that at first sight seem drab and uninteresting. But their courtship has elements that are, in some ways, even more remarkable than that of their close cousins. The bower birds' claim to fame comes from their building and decorating abilities. Most birds construct nests, but these build elaborate structures that have nothing directly to do with eggs or young. They are built by the males simply to attract a mate. The principle is the same as the gaudy plumage of the birds of paradise, but in this case the enticement is not the bird itself but an object that he has created. The bowers come in a whole range of sizes and styles. Some are merely mats of leaves and ferns arranged carefully on a cleared area of forest floor; others are avenues of sticks placed upright in parallel lines, while some are constructed as a maypole with horizontal twigs being stuck to a single vertical sapling. The most complicated of all are actually large huts, complete with roof and entrance.

These display structures are often decorated with coloured objects to make them more attractive. Fruits, flowers, stones, lichen, moss, fungi, beetle wings, snail shells and even man-made objects like buttons or bottle tops, are placed strategically on and around the bower. Different species seem to have different tastes and individual birds may develop a particular fancy for certain types of decoration. There is some evidence to suggest that females prefer objects that are naturally rare. In other words they have expensive tastes. The male has to prove that he is capable and resourceful by locating

56 PREVIOUS PAGE: *This Ulysses butterfly is just one of the great variety of large and colourful butterflies to be found in forest clearings all over New Guinea.*

57, 58 and 59 ABOVE AND LEFT: *Elaborate body decoration is a characteristic of most New Guinea societies. These faces are all from the highlands of Papua New Guinea.*

60 RIGHT: *Dancing and singing are a feature of almost all highland social occasions. These Dani warriors are engaged in a dance to celebrate victory in warfare.*

61 ABOVE: *Ritual distribution of pig meat to relatives, friends and even enemies is an important element in the politics of highland societies.*

62 ABOVE: *The ribbon-tailed*
astrapia is a bird of paradise
confined to the mountain forests that
grow just above the upper limits of
highland agriculture.

63 LEFT: *Doria's tree kangaroo lives in mountain forests and has thick fur to keep out the cold.*

64 *Macgregor's bird of paradise (ABOVE) survives only in the high subalpine forests above 3000 metres.*

65 BELOW: *Different species of animals come and go as the altitude increases. The striped possum reaches the upper limit of its range in forests just above the highland valleys.*

66 LEFT: *Mid-montane forest above Tari, in the Southern Highlands.*

67 BELOW: *The long-tailed pygmy possum lives only in mountain forests. For shelter it builds a spherical nest out of dead leaves.*

68 and 69 **LEFT AND ABOVE:** *New Guinea has over 2500 species of orchid.*

70 **BELOW:** *Boelens's python is found only in New Guinea. It survives even in the cold moss forests at an altitude of 3000 metres.*

*71 PREVIOUS PAGE: Large pockets
of open grassland are common in the
high mountains. They may have
been created by fire or by frost.*

*72 ABOVE: Subalpine forest is a
distinctive type of vegetation that
grows just below the treeline.*

*73 RIGHT: Tree ferns thrive on the
well-drained banks of highland
streams. They are amongst the most
characteristic plants of the high
mountain regions of New Guinea.*

74 ABOVE: Ok Tedi mine extracts gold, silver and copper from the remote Star Mountains of Papua New Guinea. This area remained unexplored until helicopters allowed access in the 1960s.

and retrieving objects that are difficult to find. This may explain why blue is a commonly chosen colour in bower decorations. Apart from the odd insect wing or the feathers of a few species of bird, blue is a very rare colour in the forest.

Of the eighteen species of bower bird worldwide eleven live in New Guinea. The bowers of many species are not difficult to find but the first one was not described until 1870. Some of the rarer birds were known for decades before their bower was discovered. The latest find was in 1986 when the bower of the fire-maned bower bird was located and described for the first time. Two Australians, Roy Mackay and Brian Coates, found it near a remote village in the Adelbert Mountains, inland from Madang on the north coast of Papua New Guinea. Roy described how they had picked out the village, not quite at random but certainly after a lot of guesswork, from an aerial survey. When they landed and described what they were looking for a local woman told them she knew exactly where to go, and took them directly to it the following day. Without that stroke of luck the bower of the fire-maned bower bird might have remained unknown to the outside world even today.

Male bower birds are promiscuous, just like most birds of paradise. They use the bower in the same way as a bird of paradise uses his plumes, to attract as many females as possible. There are several advantages to having a bower rather than bright feathers. For a start the bird can keep his bower from year to year, improving on it as he grows older. Birds of paradise, on the other hand, have to shed their ornamental plumage every year and grow a new set. If they did not do this it would get tatty over time. Bold and aggressive bower birds can also raid the bowers of others for building materials and decorations. It's not possible to steal feathers in the same way. When a female has been enticed in close, mating usually happens inside or near to the bower. Once fertilised the females leave, build their own nest, and rear the chicks alone.

Not all male bower birds are entirely drab or rely solely on their bowers. There seems to be a trade-off between bright feathers and a complex construction. Birds with brighter feathers build smaller structures, while the really dull ones go to fantastic lengths to create bowers of great size and complexity.

The flame bower bird, otherwise known as the golden regent

bower bird, is one of the most attractive. It has a crimson head and golden-yellow body. Its wings are also yellow but with contrasting black tips. Its bower is of the avenue type and is one of the smallest. Two lines of slender twigs stand only a few centimetres apart. They are barely taller then the bird itself and not much longer than the bird's own length. The actual display of this rare and elusive bird has not been seen but it probably involves the male passing through the avenue. He could only do this by squeezing in tightly with the walls touching him on either side. The construction is finished off with a few dark leaves and a number of berries on the floor. The combination of such a modest structure with his colourful plumage is evidently sufficient to attract the females.

In contrast, Macgregor's bower bird is dull brown, but he builds a rather more impressive construction. It includes a maypole and takes several months to complete. The male selects a slender sapling with a little space around it. He then begins to intertwine twigs so they stick out at all angles from the vertical sapling. The result is a spiny-looking pole, often about a metre in height but sometimes even taller. The twigs at the base are cut off short and the bottom of the pole packed with moss. Around this he builds a mossy runway so he can run round and round the maypole. At the edge the moss is raised into a circular wall. The bower and this wall are decorated with fruits, seeds, leaves, lichen, fungus and bits of insect cuticle. Even the surrounding vegetation is draped with decorations. Each year the male improves on the structure by extending it upwards.

Even though the bower may have been there for years and is presumably well known by females in the area, they still need enticing down. The male achieves this with a most extraordinary repertoire of calls. He whistles, screams, growls and creaks as well as imitating the sounds of frogs, insects, and even human voices. And if a female does arrive he flies to a pair of saplings, bounces vigorously from one to the other, and reveals another surprise. On the back of his head, and usually hidden, is a circular patch of bright orange feathers. He erects this crest and bobs about like a little flame in the forest. His motto seems to be 'catch me if you can'. He flies down to the track around the bower and darts round to the side opposite the female. As she moves he manoeuvres to keep hidden. Eventually, her curiosity heightened, the female herself flies down to the track and moves around it towards the male. He moves in the opposite direction, appearing to her only momentarily to give her a brief flash of his fiery crest. They dance back and forth, back and forth, the male building up the tension. But this effort may be in vain: often the female decides she has had enough and flies off, perhaps to inspect another nearby male and maypole.

As most bower birds have not been carefully studied ornithologists do not really know how important various bits of the bower are in the attraction of a mate. Does the female, for example, pay most attention to the size, or is it the shape, or perhaps the colours of the decorations? What is known is that it takes quite a lot of time for young males to get it just right, several years in fact. They often start with ineptly built bowers and include coloured decorations that are not typical for the species. But whether they simply learn by practice or from watching other males is not known.

The most impressive and complex bower of them all is built by the Vogelkop bower bird that lives only in remote and largely uninhabited mountain ranges in the north-west corner of Irian Jaya. A biologist from California, Jared Diamond, described how he had to blaze a trail in from the coast for up to twenty days to locate some of his bowers for study. In the Wandamen Mountains, where Diamond watched these birds, they build low woven towers which are covered with a massive stick hut. This is about waist high and up to 2 metres wide, with a broad entrance large enough for a child to crawl in and lie down inside. In front of this there is a 'lawn' of bright green moss. The lawn and the floor of the hut are decorated with colourful pieces of fruit, bark, flowers, fungi and insect wings.

In nearby mountains the bowers built by the same species of bird are quite different. A single bird's construction contains several tall maypoles rather like that of the Macgregor's bird in style and size. But instead of a cleared track around each maypole the whole lot is surrounded by a perfectly circular mat of dead black moss. But perhaps most remarkable of all are the decorations. *Pandanus* leaves almost 2 metres long, that's eight times longer than the bird itself, are placed up against the maypoles. Around the bower piles of hundreds of objects lie scattered about. Each pile contains just one type of decoration, whether it be snail shells or stones, acorns or beetle cuticle. The bird even paints some of those objects with a glossy black substance from its droppings. This is quite simply the most elaborately decorated structure built by any animal anywhere in the world.

The difference in design among groups of birds from the same species raises the intriguing question of whether these styles are learnt by young birds from their elders. If true, particular designs may be passed on from generation to generation by cultural transmission rather than by being rigidly imprinted in each bird's genetic make-up. After all, we pass architectural styles down through the centuries within our various cultures so why shouldn't birds?

In the forests of New Guinea one of the most plentiful sources of food is fruit. Birds of paradise and bower birds rely on it heavily, but so do others like pigeons and parrots, and therefore these two groups are also well represented on the island. But not all fruit-eating birds eat all types of fruit. Birds of paradise can tackle well-protected fruits that are rich in nutrition, probably because they were originally insect eaters, winkling grubs and beetles out of bark and rotten wood. To do this they needed to evolve powerful feet to grip the trunks of trees and a strong beak to prise away at timber. These features have then stood them in good stead when they evolved into fruit-eaters. And most birds of paradise still eat insects too, from time to time.

Fruit doves and bower birds can only tackle fruits that are rather less difficult to consume. Fortunately there are plenty of those. Some trees, like figs for example, have very accessible fruits and seem to attract just about every avian frugivore. When a single tree has a ripe crop the sight of all the different types of bird consuming a meal is a wonderful spectacle. The fruit doves alone have many different types of coats. Their names give some idea of their appearance. There are superb fruit doves, beautiful fruit doves, ornates, magnificents and even a pink spotted species.

Figs are easy targets. They are soft, juicy and unprotected. Fruit doves and bower birds tend to concentrate on this sort of meal. So does a rather unusual-looking parrot called Pesquet's parrot. It lives only in New Guinea and is now rare because it has been extensively hunted for its black and red feathers. A bare face enables it to stick its head into the biggest, juiciest fruit without getting any plumage sticky.

In all these various birds, whatever precise type of food they feed on, the fruit passes fairly swiftly through their gut. Fruit pigeons, in particular, have very short digestive tracts. The goodness is swiftly extracted and the seed passed out at the other end unharmed. That's exactly what the plant intended when it surrounded the seed in tasty flesh and coated it in a colourful and inviting skin. In this way birds get a nutritious reward for helping the plant disperse its seeds far and wide across the forest. But not all birds are as cooperative.

Parrots are specialised seed predators. Most will feed from time to time on soft fruits and their seeds, but they are also capable of opening the toughest protective covering, such as that of nuts. Perhaps the most impressive of all the parrot nut-crackers is the palm cockatoo. It lives only in the forests of New Guinea and northern Queensland. It's a large bird, almost completely black except for its cheeks which are red. On the top of its head it carries an impressive crest of feathers that can be erected at will. At the base of this crest is a huge and powerful bill. The top curves down to a sharp point while the lower mandible is short and like a chisel. With these weapons it could slice through a finger just as easily as a human being could bite through a ripe banana.

At the other end of the spectrum are parrots that consume a liquid diet. Lorikeets specialise in nectar and pollen. They are small but among the most colourful, noisy and flamboyant. They rush from tree to tree in squabbling gangs in search of freshly opened blooms. New Guinea has more species, twenty-one in all, than anywhere else. Some are common but others extremely rare, a situation not helped by the demand for unusual and colourful parrots as pets. The key to their success at feeding on flowers is their tongue. It's long and at the tip has many small, brush-like projections or papillae. When the bird is not feeding it holds these papillae in a protective sheath, but as soon as they are needed they are pushed out and expanded. They act like miniature paint brushes, soaking up nectar or pollen.

The type of food also has an impact on these birds' behaviour. Because all the flowers on a tree tend to come into bloom at once, while other trees around may have no flowers at all, large numbers of lorikeets are attracted to one spot at the same time. In such a crowd it pays to be aggressive and lorikeets certainly are. As they hop from blossom to blossom they will lunge out and display at any bird that threatens to get in their way. They tend to go round together and even roost in large flocks. Rainbow lorikeets sometimes spend the night resting in groups of thousands.

Their food is widely dispersed and unpredictable in terms of supply so they cannot establish territories like birds of paradise or bower birds. They have to roam over a wide area. They also tend to have no fixed breeding season. They just mate whenever the food supply seems plentiful. In such a variable and unstable world it's a good idea to have a permanent partner. When conditions are right it is then possible to get on and breed without having to waste time finding a mate and going through a protracted courtship ritual. In fact lorikeets pair for life.

Other New Guinea parrots have a rather different lifestyle. Pygmy parrots are the smallest parrots in the world. Some are no more than 9 centimetres long. Unlike most other parrots, they do not feed among the tree-tops. Instead they shuffle about on vertical trunks searching out tasty-looking lichen. They also eat fungus, seeds, and the odd insect. In their quick movements up vertical surfaces they resemble a treecreeper or nuthatch and, like them, they have long claws for gripping and a stiff tail to help them balance. To lay their eggs they excavate a hole in an arboreal termite nest. It isn't known if the termites provide any active protection against predators or simply provide a cosy nestbox. Groups of pygmy parrots also use these holes to roost in overnight.

The floor of the forest below also provides rich pickings; New Guinea has more than its fair share of ground-feeding birds. With no cats, foxes, or other carnivores, life on the rainforest floor is not too hazardous. Most of the marsupial predators are small and the only large ones, like the quoll, are rare. The greatest source of food for birds down here is fruit. Some falls naturally, some is dropped by flocks feeding in the canopy. The birds who take greatest advantage of this are the pigeons and doves. There are twelve different kinds that spend most of their time foraging on the ground. Some feed on seeds as well as fruit, and they do not only rely on seeds that have been directly dropped from the tree. From time to time they will visit the display court of a bird of paradise to see if he has dropped any seeds. His digestive system, unlike theirs, cannot cope with such tough items of food and he will often disgorge a seed after eating the fleshy fruit that surrounds it.

In contrast to the pretty fruit doves in the trees above, the ground-feeding species are usually dull grey and brown, although they often have a patch of iridescent colour somewhere on their bodies. Their muted coats complement their cryptic habits. Even if predators are rare, there is obviously sufficient danger on the ground for these birds to behave warily.

The crowned pigeons, on the other hand, have little to fear. They are huge, up to 80 centimetres in height, and look as plump as well-fed Christmas turkeys. These are the largest pigeons in the world. They are also some of the most spectacular. There are three species: the western, southern, and Victoria crowned pigeons. They are all confined to New Guinea and its offshore islands, and they look very similar. Their crowning glory is a delicate crest of feathers set like a lacy fan on their head. The tip of each feather in the crown is white. The rest of the fan is the same colour as the body, a subtle grey-blue. They wander round in small groups searching out fallen fruit and seeds.

Once they were quite common in lowland forests but they are a simple and tempting target for human hunters. When alarmed they will run away and only if that does not work will they take to the air. But they never fly far. Sitting on a branch in the understorey of the forest, big, fat and motionless, they make for an easy shot and a tasty and filling meal.

But not quite such a filling meal as New Guinea's biggest bird, the cassowary. The largest may be 2 metres tall and weigh 50 or 60 kilogrammes. It's not just the biggest bird on the island, it is the largest land animal of any kind in New Guinea. All three species of cassowary are flightless. Their black, glossy feathers, no longer required for flying, have evolved into a hair-like plumage that droops over their massive frame. The wings are short and stunted and the few remaining quills end in sharp points which are useful for defence and attack.

On their head and neck the feathers have disappeared completely, leaving naked skin that's coloured bright blue and red. The double wattled cassowary has a pair of long, fleshy pouches hanging from its throat. The single wattled cassowary has just one and the dwarf species has no wattles at all. On the top of their heads all cassowaries carry a huge, horn-like helmet. Just why the birds should require such a peculiar structure is something of a mystery. My favourite explanation, although I doubt if it is true, is the crash helmet theory. When a cassowary is disturbed it rushes off, barging through the undergrowth, with its body and neck held horizontally and its head jutting out in front. The theory goes that should the bird, in its panic to get away, crash into a tree the helmet would protect it. I've never heard of anyone who's seen a cassowary collide with a tree so it's rather difficult to verify this suggestion.

Cassowaries need a great deal of fallen fruit to sustain such a huge body and they wander over a large area alone, only meeting up to mate. After the female has laid her eggs she has nothing more to do with them. It is the male who sits on the nest, which is located on the ground often between the roots of a large tree. When the babies hatch they are light brown with darker stripes, perfectly camouflaged to hide among the tangled undergrowth. But they have additional protection. Their father follows the youngsters round for up to a year, giving them the benefit of his watchful eye and intimidating size.

But not all cassowary behaviour is quite as charming. They are powerful animals and, although usually shy, are very dangerous if cornered. This usually happens only with a pet or captive bird that has been pushed too far. The parts of the cassowary's anatomy that are most dangerous are the feet. The inside toe on each is elongated into a sharp spike. They attack claws first with big kicking strokes that can disembowel an enemy in no time at all. They are quite capable of tearing a man apart and people have been killed in this way.

From some of the most extravagant and beautiful to one of the most dangerous, New Guinea has a collection of birds that's amongst the most unusual in the world. They have evolved in their own unique ways because they have been isolated on an island. Freed from competition with monkeys and squirrels in the trees and with pigs and deer on the ground, the birds have been able to evolve into roles that in other forests are usually assumed by mammals. Such ecological replacement is a theme throughout much of the natural history of New Guinea.

Chapter Five

FOREST LIFE

T he island of New Guinea contains the largest expanse of undisturbed tropical rainforest in South East Asia, some 700 000 square kilometres in all. Remarkably, between 70 per cent and 80 per cent of the original forest remains intact. That's a far greater proportion than in any other part of the region.

The lowland forests contain massive trees supported by broad buttress roots. Their canopies are dense and cast deep shadows on the forest floor below. The task of escaping this gloom is the same in every tropical rainforest, and many types of plant in the under-storey are immediately recognisable to anybody who has visited similar habitats in Malaysia, The Philippines, or other tropical Asian countries. Spikes of bamboo point skyward, growing rapidly towards the sun, while *Pandanus* palms spread their slender leaves in dappled patches of light, and rattan vines wind their way through the air. Great strangler figs smother their hosts in a tangled network of roots as they struggle to maintain their position in the canopy high above.

There are, of course, some differences between these rainforests and those in neighbouring Asia. The great dipterocarp trees of the Malay Peninsula and Borneo, for example, do grow here but they are not the dominant types. Instead other genera such as *Intsia*, *Pometia*, *Alstonia* and *Vitex* are more common. A few hillsides support

unusual hoop and klinki pines. They are closely related to the
monkey puzzle tree, belonging to the same genus, *Araucaria*. Klinki
pines live only in New Guinea and are the tallest tropical trees in
the world. They tower over the canopy, reaching heights of almost
90 metres. The *Araucariae* and several other types of rainforest tree
are related to species in Australia rather than to those in Asia. There
are over 1200 species of trees in the lowland rainforest alone. On
the island as a whole there may be as many as 20 000 species of
flowering plant.

Local conditions and the island's geology have been important
in encouraging diversity. Traditionally it has been assumed that
forests are the stable end-result of a process that, left to its own
devices, tends to produce a complex web of interacting plants and
animals. Rainforests are seen as the ultimate expression of that
process: with a stable and benign climate, nature is able to diversify
into the most varied and complex habitat on earth. There is certainly
some truth in this view of the natural world. After all, a helpful
climate must surely be a prerequisite for such a rich expression of
plant life, but it is certainly not the only factor at work.

In recent years the idea that rainforest diversity is also a product
of periodic disruption, even cataclysmic destruction, has gained
favour among many ecologists. The idea is that portions of rainforest
are regularly destroyed by natural events which may range in size
from a tree falling down because of a lightning strike or old age to
whole hillsides being swept away by storms, landslides or fires.
Because the plants that are suitable for colonising these disturbed
areas of ground differ from those of the mature rainforest, over
many years the forest has become a mosaic of various types of
vegetation each in different stages of regeneration. In this way the
forest is far more diverse than it would be in a uniformly stable
state.

New Guinea is particularly prone to several kinds of natural
upheaval because of its geology, and so it is an excellent place to
investigate the theory. It is a young and highly active island, with
many steep-sided mountains and frequent volcanic eruptions.
Combine those factors with the torrential rainfall so characteristic
of the place and you have a potent recipe for landslides over much
of the landscape. From the air the frequency and extent of landslips

is very apparent. Great scars stand out on most slopes, sometimes as bare earth, but often simply as a canopy of different texture or height. In such a wet and warm environment vegetation very soon regrows and covers any newly exposed ground.

As well as landslides other powerful forces – droughts, forest fires, ash-falls from volcanoes, and the destruction and creation of land by river meanders – have also contributed to this process of dynamic regeneration. The clearing of vegetation by people practising shifting cultivation has been another important, but frequently underestimated, factor. All this disturbance combines to create a changing patchwork of vegetation. This in turn fosters tremendous diversity.

As new habitats are produced they provide fresh opportunities for animals as well as for plants. In any rainforest one group far outnumbers all the rest of them put together – the insects. New Guinea has some of the most spectacular on earth. Its forests are home to the largest of all moths, the Hercules moth. These have a wing area of over 250 square centimetres. Large size seems to be a characteristic of many New Guinea invertebrates. Giant millipedes roam the forest floor. Stick insects over 30 centimetres long hang, well camouflaged and almost invisible, on the underside of twigs. The island even has a species of fly which is known to be the widest headed fly in the world. *Achias rothschildi* can lay claim to that particular record because of its unusual eyes that stick out sideways on long stalks. This particular species has eyes so far apart that the distance between them, around 55 millimetres, is about three times greater than the length of its entire body. Only males have such extraordinary eye stalks and so it's assumed they have some sort of sexual importance, possibly as part of a courtship display.

But perhaps the most beautiful record holder among the island's insects is a butterfly. The birdwings of the genus *Ornithoptera* are the largest butterflies in the world. There are eleven or so species in all, eight of which live in New Guinea. The biggest is Queen Alexandra's birdwing which flies through the canopy on wings with a span of nearly a third of a metre. Only the females reach this size; the males are considerably smaller.

This particular species lives only in a small area of forest near the town of Popondetta on the north coast of Papua New Guinea. Why it should be confined to such a tiny section of the island is a mystery because around Popondetta it survives in a variety of habitats, many of which are also found elsewhere. Like many butterflies it is well able to make use of newly disturbed vegetation because most of the plants on which it naturally feeds thrive in the open spaces of the forest edge. But, curiously, it seems to avoid certain parts of its range which to the human observer, at least, seem ideal. Biologists obviously have a great deal to learn about the distribution and requirements of this rare butterfly, but one thing is certain, such nuances of behaviour in individual species add to the overall diversity of forest life by differentiating one species' requirements from another's.

There is a fine example of that principle at work in one of New Guinea's most unusual groups of insects, the antlered flies. They are so named because of the large antler-like structures that protrude from the heads of the males. There are only six species in the world. One lives in northern Queensland, the rest in New Guinea. Females lay their eggs under the bark of rotting wood. The crucial point is that each species of fly lays its eggs in a different kind of rotting tree. Without their own particular types of tree they could not survive. Why each species of fly has become so specialised that it requires a certain type of wood is still unknown, but it serves to demonstrate how tiny differences in behaviour can restrict individual species to a particular niche in the forest. It is also another example of the importance of disturbance in creating new opportunities, and hence contributing to the overall diversity of life in the forest. Without fallen trees rotting on the forest floor there simply would not be any antlered flies at all because they would have nowhere to lay their eggs.

Having such restricted sites for egg-laying has other consequences for these strange animals. Appropriate patches of rotting wood are rare and males try to defend them from rivals so they can mate with any females coming to lay their eggs. To do this they have evolved the huge antlers that grow from the side of their heads. They use these great appendages to demonstrate their size and strength to other males, and in some species they actually wield them as weapons to fight off competitors, rather like rutting stags. Once a male has successfully secured a good site he can be sure of fertilising any females that arrive to lay their eggs there.

The forests of New Guinea also supply a range of specialised homes for insects. The island has a great variety of plants in the genera *Myrmecodia* and *Hydnophytum*. These maintain a very special relationship with ants and are commonly called ant-plants. They are epiphytes, growing not on the ground but on the trunks of trees. They look like large warty blisters with a few leaves sprouting from the side. Unlike true parasites they do not obtain nutrition directly from their host tree but rely instead on their ants.

As it germinates from seed each plant develops a series of interconnected hollow chambers inside a huge tuber. These provide a home for certain species of ants which, in return for shelter, provide nutrition for the plant. Not all the rooms in their lodgings are the same. Some are smooth and provide the actual living quarters; in others the walls have small protuberances and in these chambers the insects deposit their droppings, scraps of food and the bodies of any ants that die within the colony. They also inoculate these heaps of rotting detritus with fungal spores which eventually develop into fungus gardens tended by the ants. As all this organic matter mulches down it is absorbed by the plant through the warty lumps on the walls of the chambers.

Sometimes other less welcome animals take advantage of the available room space. During our filming in Papua New Guinea we found a tiny snake hiding in an ant-plant tuber. Biologist Matthew Jebb, who has made an extensive study of New Guinea ant-plants, has even found a tiny frog, *Cophixalus riparius*, using the ants' living quarters as a nest-hole. The chambers sometimes fill with rainwater and the frogs then lay their eggs inside.

The plants and animals of the forest interact in many ways that are mutually beneficial. One of the most widespread and important functions animals perform for rainforest plants is pollination. In countries with a temperate climate we are used to thinking of insects as the main pollinators of flowers. In the rainforest they also have a vital part to play. Each species of fig, for example, has its own species of tiny fig wasp that carries its pollen from one tree to the next. But in rainforests there are many other animals able to pollinate flowers.

Birds that feed on flowers are an obvious possibility and in the lorikeets New Guinea has its very own range of small pollen and nectar-feeding parrots. As their brush-like tongues lap up pollen they are almost certain to transfer some of it to their next feeding site and thus help the plants cross-pollinate themselves. Likewise sunbirds and several species of honeyeater also perform the same function.

While flowers pollinated by insects and birds tend to be brightly coloured to attract the appropriate animals, this is not much use to nocturnal creatures. Flowers pollinated by bats tend to be rather dull, often attracting the bats by smell instead.

A further problem is positioning the flowers so that they can be approached easily by a flying mammal that may be relatively heavy. The solution for many trees which rely on bat pollination is to produce flowers growing directly from their trunk. This provides a firm landing pad for the bats. Others hold their flowers out on lengthy but strong stalks, well away from potentially entangling leaves and branches. Bananas, of which there are many wild species in New Guinea, do this. Their large bulbous flower buds hang far out on stems that may be a metre or more long. As dusk approaches their protective covering peels back to reveal several trumpet-like flowers surrounding a solid core which shields yet more flowers that will be exposed on another night. This large bulbous core provides an ideal surface on which small blossom bats can get a good grip.

Some of the marsupials also pollinate rainforest flowers. In Varirata National Park possums have been observed pollinating a leguminous vine. Sugar gliders also visit flowers and frequently feed on nectar and pollen, so they also probably have a part to play.

Just as pollination by animals is vital to create new life in the forest, animals are also important in clearing up and recycling the mess after forest vegetation has died. In New Guinea there are some rather unusual scavengers. Wandering through almost any patch of lowland forest, you are quite likely to trip over small mounds of earth with neat circular holes at their centre. During the day their occupants remain underground, it is only as darkness descends that their identity is revealed. The first part of the body to emerge has no fur or feathers on it; in fact it's a large horny claw, for the owners of these holes are crabs. They are common throughout the lowlands of New Guinea and are important in breaking down dead vegetation. Some species lay their eggs in forest streams and pools while others that live near the coast need to return to the sea to deposit their eggs.

Other creatures active in the forest at night that usually require water for their eggs are frogs. They are far more obvious than the crabs because they are so noisy. Just after dusk the air is filled with a great cacophony of cheeping, trilling, piping and croaking. Tracking down individual frogs by their calls can be frustrating. Most of the noise is produced by males trying to attract a mate. Presumably females must be able to find them easily, but to human ears the sounds can often be difficult to locate. One group of New Guinea frogs poses a particular problem. They emit a loud, low-frequency call and, in theory, it ought to be easy to track them down, but it's always impossible to find the frog because they are hidden underground.

These frogs belong to a group called the microhylids. Not all of them live underground, by any means, but those that do are well adapted for burrowing. Their bodies are fat and rounded with small limbs, while their skulls are reinforced and often pointed for shoving head-first through the soil. Their eyes are small and retractable and the skin on the snout is designed to be rapidly replaced if it's abraded away. Their calls are also well suited for an underground life and are quite different from those of related species living above the surface. Sounds of high frequency are rapidly muted by passing through solid matter and so these underground frogs have very deep voices that carry well through soil and leaf litter.

It is not known exactly why they live beneath the surface of the earth. Most burrowing frogs in the rest of the world do so to avoid desiccation. They tend to live in deserts and arid places and spend much of their lives cocooned underground to prevent moisture loss. They only emerge after rains. With rainfall here so plentiful the ground is almost permanently damp, which is ideal for frogs. There does not seem to be a good functional reason for them to need to burrow underground, but the subsoil does provide protection and a plentiful supply of invertebrate food. There are vast numbers of different types of frogs in rainforest, over 200 species in New Guinea alone, and they are all competing for survival. It may simply be that living space is crowded and with an underground niche available it is bound to be filled by something. If so, it's yet another example of the way in which the forest is divided up to provide a great range of small, specialised habitats.

One of the most distinctive features of microhylids in New Guinea is the absence of a tadpole stage in their life history. In other words they are frogs that do not need ponds or streams in which to lay their eggs. Why these microhylids have dispensed with the tadpole stage seems as puzzling as the burrowing. After all, there are plenty of streams and ponds in which eggs can be laid and in which tadpoles could survive. Perhaps part of the reason is that the forest is just so damp there is simply no necessity to put eggs into water in the first place because they are able to survive in the humid atmosphere without drying out. For added protection they are usually laid inside the stems or among the furled-up leaves of plants. Each female produces only a few eggs at a time – fifty at the most. Males call to prospective mates from suitable egg-laying sites and once the clutch is laid they often remain to protect it. The eggs themselves are very yolky and contain sufficient nutrients for the developing young to grow into baby frogs without the need to feed. This is a fascinating process to watch because the froglets are clearly visible inside the transparent eggs. They squirm around, moving fairly actively for several days, before eventually hatching as fully formed minia-ture frogs.

The other major group of frogs in New Guinea are the Hylidae or tree frogs, although not all of them live in trees. All except one species lay their eggs in water and produce true tadpoles. But having a normal life history does not necessarily mean that things are straightforward. Although heavy rainfall produces forest conditions that are moist, and hence ideal for amphibians, it also creates streams that are often swollen and fast-flowing. That brings prob-lems for courting males. When attracting a mate it's important for the male to be close to an egg-laying site if he is going to have a chance of fertilising a female's eggs. If this happens to be a fast flowing stream his voice might well be drowned out by the sound of the water.

Dr James Menzies, from the University of Papua New Guinea, has recorded the calls of several species of hylid that habitually live in streamside vegetation. They are rather distinctive. Dr Menzies describes them as metallic ringing sounds that seem to contain a very narrow band of frequencies. But those frequencies they do have tend to be different from those given off by the neighbouring stream. By tuning into the particular frequencies used by the males the females may be able to screen out much of the unwanted and distracting water noise. Even to the human ear they are distinctly audible in among the sounds of rushing water.

Fast streams also present another problem: eggs and tadpoles can easily be swept away. Several New Guinea frogs manage to overcome this by modifications to their eggs and tadpoles. In *Nyctimystes* species, most of which breed in flowing water, the eggs are large and sticky, and tend to remain together in a clump. Their tadpoles are strong, with flattened bodies and powerful sucker mouths. They are able to cling onto rocks to prevent themselves from being swept downstream.

In all rainforests around the world there are similar opportunities to be exploited and animals tend to evolve in ways that enable them to make the best of these. Consequently, unrelated animals in different parts of the world sometimes evolve to look and behave more or less the same. New Guinea has many such examples of parallel evolution because the selection of animals it started out with was relatively restricted. Snakes are among the most important predators on the island because there are no large carnivorous animals in these forests.

Not all groups are represented in New Guinea. Snakes are very specialised reptiles and evolved relatively late in evolutionary history, after the supercontinent of Gondwana had broken up. To reach New Guinea meant crossing the sea. The ancestors of elapids, such as cobras and coral snakes, were able to make this journey, but for some unknown reason those of the adders and vipers were unable to do so.

As a result the ecological space occupied by vipers elsewhere on earth has not been taken up by them here. But it has not remained vacant, because one of the elapids, the death adder, has evolved to fill that role. It is not an adder but just looks and behaves like one. It has a short, stout viper-like body and a wide viper-like head. Above each eye it has a long raised scale that is similar in appearance to the 'horns' of some vipers. But the similarity does not stop with appearance. Just like vipers, death adders use their cryptic colouration to remain hidden from prey, but when they strike they do so suddenly. That makes them especially dangerous to people. They are nocturnal and lie around during the day. When approached they tend not to move, presumably hoping they will not be spotted, but if they are accidentally stepped on they will attack and bite swiftly. Some real vipers twitch their tail to attract unsuspecting prey, such as small lizards, to within reach, and the New Guinea death adder also does the same. And like many true vipers female death adders give birth to live young rather than laying eggs. The similarities in these two completely unrelated types of snake are remarkable, but they are not the only such examples.

New Guinea has a good selection of pythons, eight species in all, and one is particularly attractive, the green tree python. It bears a startling resemblance to the South American emerald tree boa. In fact so similar are the two species that if they are kept together in a zoo it is virtually impossible for the untrained eye to tell them apart. Not only are the adults almost identical in appearance but the youngsters of both species go through a similar colour change as they grow older.

Baby green tree pythons are born bright yellow or orange but after several months turn green. This can happen rapidly, in as little as two days, for a complete colour change. Emerald tree boas are also born orange and turn green as they grow older. Why both species undergo such a remarkable transition is as yet unknown. It might be something to do with camouflage and the different habitats that juveniles and adults occupy, or something to do with social behaviour. But even more puzzling than the change itself is the mystery of why two unrelated species, separated by many thousands of kilometres of Pacific Ocean, should have skin colour that behaves in exactly the same way. Both snakes are arboreal hunters and catch birds, frogs and lizards. They both have prehensile tails to help them climb and when at rest both coil themselves around a branch in a characteristic posture. These two animals are one of the most startling examples of natural selection creating similar features in different animals, simply because they live in the same type of habitat and share the same lifestyles.

Because the island is missing certain kinds of animals its forests originally had several ecological gaps. This has allowed a few types of animal, that elsewhere are adapted for a particular way of life, to diversify into a whole range of lifestyles not typical of their group. Kingfishers, for example, are found almost everywhere in the world and New Guinea is no exception. They are usually associated with water but in New Guinea they have evolved to make their living through a whole variety of activities, many of which no longer rely on water.

A few species, like the common and the little kingfisher, still catch fish as the main element in their diet. But most others prey on insects, spiders, centipedes and even small vertebrates like lizards, frogs and snakes. These forest birds do, however, still hunt in the typical kingfisher way – waiting motionless on an exposed perch before diving down on their prey. Most attack their victims on foliage or the ground, but some, the dwarf kingfisher is an example, catch dragonflies and other insects on the wing. One species, the shovel-billed kingfisher, has even abandoned the habit of perching and waiting. It now hunts by digging into the forest floor, unearthing arthropods, earthworms, snails, even snakes. Yet another species, the hook-billed kingfisher, has become nocturnal, hunting mainly at night.

Some of the fishing species still nest in burrows dug in river banks, but others excavate nest holes, either in rotting tree stumps or in large termite nests. Most of the latter are attached to the sides of trees, but one bird, the white-tailed paradise kingfisher, specialises in nesting in termite nests on the ground.

The twenty-two species of kingfisher living in New Guinea are just one fascinating example of how animals and plants have evolved to occupy the variety of potential lifestyles offered by the island's rainforests. That they and many other species have done so in an unconventional way is related to New Guinea's position in the world. It has received a selection of immigrants from both Asia and Australia, resulting in an unusual mix of life to start with. On top of that it is an island, allowing its fauna and flora to evolve in comparative isolation from the rest of the world. These two factors have contributed to the bizarre character of much of New Guinea's natural history.

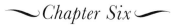
SOUTHERN SAVANNAS

Not all the lowlands of New Guinea are covered in dense jungle or swamp. Along its southern border the island has several patches of grassy plain and open woodland. Some extend back from the coast for over 100 kilometres, others for less than 30. During the driest part of the year little if any rain falls here. Most other habitats on the island have no such periods of drought and remain lush and green all year round, but these savannas endure the fierce rays of the tropical sun without respite, often for several months. They become yellow, shrivelled and parched. A searing haze of heat shimmers just above the ground and when the wind blows it feels like the exhaust from a furnace – hot and desiccating. A strike of rogue lightning or the spark from a man-made fire can swiftly grow into a ferocious sheet of flames that leaves the landscape black and charred. Life here is a world away from the jungles and mountains that cover most of New Guinea. The scenery is more reminiscent of the African savanna or the Australian outback.

Most of these savanna areas experience a monsoon type climate, with a wet as well as a dry season. During the wet season rains are heavy. Seasonal inundation is common, especially near the rivers that meander over the plains. In places that experience alternating floods and dry spells wildlife is especially plentiful and conspicuous.

The largest such area straddles the border between Papua New Guinea and Irian Jaya on the southern coast of the island. It's a vast plain created over several thousand years by the deltas of south flowing rivers. On the Papua New Guinea side the plains are within the Tonda Wildlife Management Area. Only local people are allowed to exploit the wildlife freely. Outsiders have to pay a licence fee to visit the area for fishing, hunting and tourism. The seasonally flooded savanna along the Bensbach River is a particularly popular spot for visitors because of its bird life. In Irian Jaya part of the plains are preserved in the Wasur Wildlife Reserve, upgraded to National Park status in 1991. That both countries have in theory decided to protect some of the area is an indication of its unique nature when compared with the habitats that cover the rest of the island.

Only a few thousand years ago these areas of savanna were part of a great plain that stretched all the way to Australia over what is now the Torres Strait. During the past two million years global ice ages have, on several occasions, lowered sea levels sufficiently to create such land-bridges. At those times the fauna and flora of New Guinea and Australia intermixed freely. Rising seas finally separated them just 8000 years ago. Today the strait that keeps them apart is only 150 kilometres wide and in most places less than 50 metres deep. The natural history on both sides still has much in common.

Much of the wildlife in the savanna is actually identical with that on the neighbouring continent of Australia. This is not a coincidence. Across New Guinea as a whole many of the animals and plants are similar to those in Australia because they share a common ancestry. But they are not exactly the same because most have adapted to a rainforest existence, while those in Australia have evolved to cope with drier conditions. These areas of grass and woodland, however, have the same sort of climate as that in northern Australia, to which they are so close. The result is that the southern savannas retain many species *identical* with those on the continent to the south.

Those that instantly give the savanna a truly Australian feel are the large hopping marsupials. New Guinea has none of the largest kangaroos but these grassy plains do support herds of agile wallabies. They hang around in groups of up to a dozen, occasionally more in places where the grazing is particularly good. In Australia they are nervous animals always looking around to spot approaching danger. When especially worried they thump their feet on the ground, presumably as a warning to others in their group. On the Bensbach plains, where there are very few human beings to disturb them, the animals are remarkably tame, and curious as well.

During the driest part of the year they venture out to graze in the early morning, but later in the day take shelter from the burning sun under the shade of nearby trees. They have a rather curious way of cooling off. They lick their forearms until they are thoroughly wet and then hold them out to catch the breeze. As the saliva evaporates from their fur it cools the blood passing close to the surface of their skin. When this flows around the rest of the body it cools other parts too.

Mother wallabies, and many other female kangaroos too, have the unusual ability to support simultaneously three young, each at different stages of development. As soon as a joey leaves the pouch, at about seven or eight months, its mother gives birth to another baby. This will have been lying dormant as an embryo within her womb and only begins to resume growth once the pouch is free. Soon after the birth the female remates and another embryo develops up to a certain stage inside her and then stops growing, a phenomenon known as embryonic diapause. So the mother is supporting an embryo, a joey in her pouch, and another youngster at her feet all at the same time. The oldest youngster continues to suckle after leaving the pouch. Its mother produces different milk out of each teat, one sort for the joey, another for the older animal. This sophisticated reproductive system means that females are continuously pregnant throughout life. There are definite advantages to this. If any of her young offspring should die a mother wallaby always has another on the way. Any breeding setbacks are therefore only temporary.

Tall termite mounds are typical of both the Australian bush and these southern savannas in New Guinea. They provide a rich feast for the short-beaked echidna. These are stocky animals with coarse brown hair and long spines, not unlike large hedgehogs at first sight. They are monotremes, unusual egg-laying mammals related to the duck-billed platypus. In the past Australia and New Guinea each had two types. Judging by the biology of their modern relatives, the short-beaked echidnas inhabited a variety of habitats and fed on ants and termites, while the long-beaked ones (also known as giant spiny anteaters; see chapter 3) lived mainly in damp, mountain forests and thrived on worms. Today Australia has very little moist forest and long-beaked echidnas no longer survive there. They remain only in the tropical rainforests of New Guinea, but their smaller relative still thrives in the Australian bush and is the very same species as the animal that now lives on these southern savannas.

Echidnas have often been described as primitive mammals because of their egg-laying habits and other features that seem to link them with birds and reptiles. But they are far from primitive. They have brains that are not only comparatively large for the size of the animal but which also contain many convolutions on their surface. These folds and ridges increase the surface area of the brain and are generally associated with high mental ability in mammals. Tests of their intelligence have proved them to be at least as bright as domestic cats. They are also highly successful ecologically, being the most widespread of any mammal in Australasia. All an echidna seems to need is a plentiful supply of ants or termites.

In New Guinea it is a nocturnal hunter, finding its prey by smell. Once it has located a promising termite or ant nest it uses powerful forepaws to dig inside, and then extricates the insects with an astonishingly long and sticky tongue. In some animals this can be up to 17 centimetres from base to tip, over a third the length of its body. Having no teeth to chew with, the echidna also has to use its tongue to masticate food. At the back of the tongue is a horny pad with which insect prey can be ground against a similar surface on the roof of the mouth. If attacked while out foraging away from its lair, an echidna can either roll into a ball like a hedgehog or bury itself rapidly, with its spines giving overhead protection.

As well as the Australian mammals it supports, the savanna is also home for several distinctive grassland birds that originate from Australia. The Australian bustard is one of the most striking. This is a large game bird that stands a metre or more high. Although it can fly well on powerful, rounded wings it spends most of the time on the ground hunting for insects and other small animals. The male has a spectacular courtship display in which he puffs out a huge white-feathered throat sac. This is so large it hangs nearly to the ground and acts as a powerful resonating chamber for his voice. He struts round and round, droops his wings, bends his tail up over his back, and calls loudly to impress rivals and potential mates alike. These plains are the only place in New Guinea where this Australian species breeds.

Another large Australian bird that also reproduces on these savanna grasslands and has an impressive display is the Brolga crane. These are elegant grey birds with a splash of red on the sides and back of the head. They often congregate in groups and sometimes in flocks of up to several hundred strong. Their dances happen at any time of year, although they are more frequent at the start of the breeding season. A bird leaps into the air, often having plucked a clump of vegetation that it then throws and catches in its bill. As it jumps it spreads both wings out wide and maintains this position while repeatedly bouncing up and down.

The open woodlands that fringe the plains are also Australian in appearance. That's hardly surprising as many of the trees are *Eucalyptus* species. *Acacias* are also common. In the wetter areas, where water remains for most of the year, one of the most typical trees is the *Melaleuca* or paperbark, so called because the bark flakes away in paper-like strips. It's ideally adapted to this seasonally flooded habitat and can survive months of being waterlogged. It has a second set of roots part of the way up the tree that help it to breathe while floodwaters cover the base of the trunk and the underground roots.

The rains are the key to the rhythm of life here. As the dry season comes to a close the plains are yellow and dry and the rivers well below their banks. It is possible to drive for miles in any direction on the flat surface, with virtually no obstructions blocking the way. Herds of wallabies are spread out over the landscape at this time of year, looking for the best remaining grass. They are joined in their grazing by Rusa Deer, introduced in the 1920s by the Dutch and now established as a large population over half a million strong. These two species between them have mown the plains down to a short sward during the dry season.

As storms build up over the distant mountains to the north the trickle of water in the rivers swells to a surge. It rises higher and higher until eventually it breaks their banks and sends water swilling over hundreds of square kilometres of savanna. From a dry and dusty plain the landscape is transformed, effectively, into a lake. Many of the animals have to take shelter on any piece of higher ground they can find or else they must disperse into the forests beyond the edge of the grassland. This dramatic annual transition makes it very difficult for people to live here permanently which is one of the reasons human population levels are so low and why animal life is still so abundant.

One group of animals finds the combination of wet and dry no problem at all. In fact they thrive on it. Monitors are the largest of all lizards. With a tough skin that resists desiccation and stout legs that allow them to walk well on land, they cope superbly with the dry season. Some species can stand up on their hind legs to give themselves a better view over the long grass, and some can even run on them. Gould's monitor is reputed to be able to outrun a person over short distances. But in the wet season they are equally at home in the water: most are strong swimmers. To rest, or to survey their surroundings, they are easily able to climb out of the water into bushes or up the trunks of trees.

With such versatile behaviour and no large mammalian carnivores with which to compete (except for dogs, introduced by man), they are the dominant meat-eaters of this world. They track their prey with long and mobile tongues; monitors are the only lizards with forked tongues. These flicker from between their lips, collecting airborne chemicals which are then transferred for analysis to a special sense organ at the back of the mouth called Jacobson's organ. Both these features are similar to those in snakes. Like snakes, monitors also have thin, fang-like teeth with sharp cutting edges. These are designed not for chewing but for holding struggling prey which are then swallowed whole, or at least in large chunks. But in spite of their large size, savage appearance and sharp teeth, they seem happier scavenging from a rotting corpse than catching large live prey.

In the woods that surround these grasslands lives Salvadori's monitor lizard. Its claim to fame is that it is the longest lizard in the world. The Komodo dragon from Indonesia is heavier and more massive but Salvadori's monitor exceeds it in length. Local people say it can grow to at least 5 metres in length, although most of that would be tail. Locally it's known as 'puk puk bilong tri' which means crocodile that lives in the trees, and it's certainly a good climber.

The annual inundation that changes the landscape so dramatically also brings with it rich sediment to fertilise the floodplain. The grasses and other plants receive a great boost and this in turn helps the fish life. While the water covers the land fish and eels move out from the rivers to feed and breed in the expanse of shallow water. The plentiful aquatic life supports large populations of both plant and flesh-eating animals. None are more conspicuous than birds.

The concentration of birds varies with the changing seasons. Some stay all year round, but many migrate from Australia, spending just a few months here before returning. It's only a short aerial hop and at certain times of year conditions are better here than further south, especially if there's a drought in Australia. The sodden and flooded grass makes a great meal for thousands of magpie geese, so called because of their black and white colour which is not unlike the markings on a magpie. This seasonal swampland is the only place they are found in New Guinea. They feed on grasses and other plants both in and out of the water. Should they be disturbed, perhaps by a wedge-tailed eagle flying overhead, they rise in such clouds that they seem to block out almost all the sky.

The whistling duck is another herbivorous water bird that congregates here in vast numbers. Large flocks of them can be seen on dry strips of ground during the day. They seem to move as one super-organism, with waves of activity passing from one side of the flock to the other. They feed only occasionally during daylight hours and are most active at night when they dabble and dive for nutritious water plants.

The area is also important as a staging post for migrant waders flying between breeding grounds in Asia and wintering sites in Australia. The birds probe the mud around the edge of pools for invertebrate food, topping up their energy reserves before continuing their long journeys. Birds of several species often forage together. Mongolian plovers, common greenshanks, sharp-tailed sandpipers, long-toed stints and curlew sandpipers all join mixed species flocks. The numbers of individual species can be impressive. In one season over 10 000 little curlews have been recorded passing through on their journey from Siberia to northern Australia. That's a considerable proportion of the entire world population.

As the water begins to recede during the dry season the pools of water shrink in size. The timing of this varies from year to year. Sometimes it happens in June, but in other years the plains are still deep in water into September. At this time all the birds become concentrated at these rich feeding grounds. It is by far the best time of year for bird watching, but the only way to get a really good view of them is to be up before sunrise and into a hide close to one of the remaining lagoons.

As dawn breaks pelicans are often among the first birds to arrive. They glide down in formation out of the grey morning sky. Extending their feet as water skis, they skid across the surface of the lagoon in a shower of spray before finally coming to a halt. These are Australian pelicans and they come over here mainly during the wet season. Pelicans are not after plants; they are hunters and hunt in teams. As the water levels fall fish and eels become trapped in the last few remaining pools. At times the water surface literally seems to writhe with life. To concentrate the food even further the pelicans swim together in a curved line pushing the fish before them. In unison they duck their heads and fill their large throat pouches with wriggling food.

Other hunters use different techniques. Around the edges of the pools large numbers of herons and egrets gather. They catch their prey by individual stealth, although in these rich waters simply stabbing out in any direction seems to achieve results. The eels seem almost as long as the birds themselves, but the birds always seem to manage. The herons and egrets are joined by flocks of white and glossy ibis, and royal spoonbills trawling the water for smaller prey. Cormorants, darters, and grebes hunt underwater, then suddenly appear at the surface with fish in their mouths. Black-necked storks strut along the water's edge. Overhead, groups of whiskered terns hover and dive. The scene is one of activity, bordering on chaos. It is as though the birds know the food supply will not last for long, so they must make the most of it while they can.

For the trapped fish and eels there is no escape, and as the pools dry up many simply die through lack of oxygen. When a large catfish is left gasping for breath in the shallows it makes an irresistible meal for birds of prey. Whistling kites are common here, as they are over much of the lowlands of New Guinea. They are often to be seen tearing at the carcasses of fish on the edge of lagoons. Even the large white-bellied fish eagles take carrion rather than hunting when the opportunity presents itself. At this time of year stranded fish attract a variety of scavengers and a kite or eagle may have to defend its meal against the unwanted attention of a monitor lizard or even a pair of hungry crows. Fortunately, not all the fish get trapped in the evaporating pools. Some remain in the rivers and survive until the following year to breed and build up populations once again.

Not all the grasslands and open woodlands of southern New Guinea are regularly flooded in this way. In fact a narrow coastal strip of grass and woodland that extends as far east as Port Moresby and beyond, is the driest part of the entire island. Naturally it does not support large flocks of water birds as the Bensbach plains do, but many of the same animals do survive here, although often in smaller numbers because of the denser human population. Wallabies, for example, are hunted and so tend to be nocturnal. Neither do they live in large, conspicuous herds. Poisonous snakes live in both places and seem to survive in spite of people.

Australia has one of the deadliest collections of venomous reptiles in the world and these strips of grass and woodland contain several of them. Like Australia, New Guinea has no vipers; all the poisonous snakes are elapids. Perhaps the most dangerous snake in all Australia, and the Pacific too, is the taipan. New Guinea has a subspecies of its own that lives only in these southern savannas. The taipan has one of the deadliest venoms known of any snake in the world. It contains a powerful neurotoxin that interferes with nerve endings, preventing them functioning properly. Only 7 or 8 milligrams is sufficient to kill a human within a few hours and a large taipan can deliver well over ten times that amount in a single bite.

The snake grows up to 4 metres in length and is a fast mover, but it is shy and tends to avoid people. With well-developed senses of smell and sight it usually manages to do this very effectively. Only if surprised will it attack, but if it does it will be with great speed and aggression. Inevitably there are many local stories about the fierceness of these snakes, including several tales of people being chased by them. Fortunately the truth is quite different. If it were not timid and retiring it could create havoc in the grasslands of New Guinea.

In parts of southern New Guinea the Papuan black snake, or 'pap black' as it's commonly known, seems to be feared even more. It lives in the same grassland habitat as the taipan but seems to like slightly damper areas too and will also venture into forests. The New Guinea species has a venom that is twice as toxic as that of its Australian relatives, although it is not as powerful as the taipan's. The pap black isn't a common snake and is rarely seen. Sightings are even less frequent than they might be because of the snake's behaviour. It is very nervous and tends to flee at the first indication of an approaching human being, but it is regarded by local people as a deadly, almost supernatural foe. Its jet black colour may be responsible for this attitude, or perhaps it is because when cornered and molested it will attack with a ferocity greater than any other snake on the island. Whatever the reason, the discovery of any black snake in the Port Moresby area is likely to cause almost hysterical panic.

Not all the snakes found in these areas are potentially deadly. The commonest of all is the brightly coloured carpet python that lives around Port Moresby and on the plains that straddle the Irian Jaya–Papua New Guinea border, as well as in parts of Australia too. It comes out mainly at night to hunt rodents. In this way it is of considerable help to the local human population, but, in spite of this, it is still widely persecuted and deliberately killed, as well as frequently being squashed by vehicles on the road.

Not all reptiles that look like snakes are snakes. One charming little creature living in these grasslands of which this is true is the legless lizard. At first sight it certainly looks like a snake: it is long and thin and squirms through the grass. But its head is fine and delicate, and when it licks its lips it is not with a forked tongue but with a broad flat one. It is actually a lizard that, through evolution, has lost the need for legs. This does not seem to impede its hunting ability. It can propel its body forward without actually seeming to move at all, creeping forward until its jaws are close to its prey, and then it strikes with lightning speed.

These grasslands and open woodlands that today support such a distinct collection of reptiles, mammals and birds are the result of the special climatic conditions experienced by the southernmost parts of the island. A pronounced dry season has been especially crucial. But elsewhere are grasslands with a different origin. They have been created over the past several thousand years by mankind, often using fire. The main reasons for burning and transforming the landscape in this way have been the clearing of land for crops and the flushing out of game for hunting. The arrival of mankind and its early impact on the environment are the subject of the next chapter.

Chapter Seven

THE ARRIVAL
of MAN

*O*ver the past few hundred thousand years the earth has been through many dramatic changes. The most important of these, as far as animals and plants are concerned, have been the waxing and waning of successive ice ages. As each new wave of glaciation began the temperature of the whole world fell and huge sheets of ice formed in the most northerly and southerly latitudes. Even the tropics did not escape. Right on the equator great glaciers grew on the mountain summits. With so much water locked up in ice sheets and glaciers sea levels dropped by more than 100 metres. Where previously there had been ocean, land appeared.

During the past hundred millennia such a scenario has repeated itself on three major occasions. During these periods the waters around the world have been so low that many previously isolated pieces of land became linked together by dried-up sea bed. New Guinea, for example, has been connected to northern Australia. To its west many of the islands of the Indonesian archipelago – Bali, Java, Sumatra and Borneo – have been attached to South East Asia. But the stretch between New Guinea and Asia is one strip of water that has never dried up. Throughout geological time this has kept many Asian animals, especially mammals, out of New Guinea. Apart from bats and rats and mice, only one other mammal made it across the sea. That mammal was man.

Evidence of the earliest human arrivals is difficult to find because many of the places where people might first have settled, along the shores of the island, have since been destroyed by the forces of nature. At the end of the last ice age, around 10 000 years ago, sea levels rose dramatically. Most coastal sites inhabited by people before that period would have been covered by the rising seawater. At the same time, any remains of human activity and habitation along river banks would have been either eroded away or smothered in silt as new deltas began to form. As a result, most of the evidence of early human settlement on New Guinea has been covered over or otherwise obliterated.

But on the Huon Peninsula massive geological forces have been lifting the coast up faster than sea levels have been rising. The most visible proof of that are ancient coral reefs that now sit on hillsides, high above the modern shoreline. Because of that fortuitous situation evidence of coastal occupation by early human settlers has been lifted clear of the sea and has been preserved. It shows that human beings made the journey to New Guinea very early indeed. Archaeologists have unearthed stone axes 40 000 years old. To put that in perspective, modern man did not invade Europe until about 5000 years later. So people managed to invade the island of New Guinea right at the dawn of modern man's worldwide expansion.

At that time sea levels were lower than now and the gap to the islands of the Indonesian archipelago was shorter. The distance that people would have had to travel across the sea was still probably no less than 100 kilometres. That was quite a feat so early in human prehistory. These may well have been the world's first seafarers. People did not manage to navigate over much shorter stretches of water in the Mediterranean for another 30 000 years, when many of the Greek islands were settled.

How the first people came to New Guinea 40 000 or more years ago is not known. Being so far in the past it is likely to remain one. There is certainly no evidence from anywhere in the world that boats or sailing vessels had been developed so long ago. But that may simply reflect the fact that remains of such wooden vessels would probably have rotted away by now anyway. In the absence of any clues most archaeologists assume that these early seafarers must have travelled on simple rafts.

When they arrived on the island the world they found would have been, in many ways, similar to the one they had left. They were almost certainly coastal dwellers already used to making a living from coral reefs and lagoons. These new waters would have been full of edible animals familiar to them. They would not have required any special equipment to catch a meal because many reef animals can be collected easily by hand, especially if the collector knows where to look. Such gathering of seafood is called gleaning and can be a valuable source of protein. It is still practised today along the coasts of New Guinea.

In Port Moresby, the capital city of Papua New Guinea, the downtown area of banks and general stores sits on a rocky headland fringed by coral reefs. Whenever I drove past this area and the tide was low I noticed dozens of women and children picking their way over the reef table. When the water is low this is only a few centimetres below the surface. The people were shuffling forward slowly while peering intently into the sea. They were searching for molluscs, sea shells, and other small invertebrates. Individually they are not big, but they are not difficult to gather either and a few handfuls make a very nutritious meal.

The waters around the island contained larger animals too. Apart from fish, which occur in great variety, there were dolphins, dugong and turtles. The first two are difficult to hunt, but turtles require no special techniques. For the early human settlers, and for coastal people in New Guinea today, they can provide a very substantial and easy catch. Because they have to come out on land to lay their eggs they are extremely vulnerable at certain times of year and the eggs themselves are an additional and tasty bonus. Six of the seven species of marine turtles live in these waters. But turtles can provide more than just food, and as time passed people learned to use the shells too. These can be fashioned into combs, spoons, knives, pins and many other useful household items. Hawksbill turtleshell, because of its beauty, has been prized until very recently for the manufacture of bracelets, earrings and other jewellery.

Many of the plants growing on the shore would also have been very familiar to the earliest human settlers. The forests of New Guinea share many of the same types of trees, palms, herbs and other plants with forests in South East Asia, and many can be eaten.

In fact this Malesian flora has a greater number of species useful to man than any other region on earth. In New Guinea there are wild *Pandanus* and *Barringtonia* trees with nutritious nuts, several species of wild banana and ginger, as well as edible sago, sugar cane, pit-pit, giant swamp taro and yam. Today over 200 different types of native plant are used as food.

But the newly arrived inhabitants of the island did not merely hunt and gather the products of the seas and forests. They began to mould their local environment. We know this because of those 40 000-year-old stone axes. They were found by Dr Les Groube, a former lecturer at the University of Papua New Guinea, during several expeditions to the Huon Peninsula in the 1980s.

The axes are large, some weighing 2 kilogrammes, and have been fashioned with a waist in their middle. This waist was almost certainly there to allow a haft to be bound on to the stone, enabling the axe to be swung with some force. Yet despite this sophistication (these may be the earliest hafted axes anywhere in the world), the cutting edges were not very hard. People could not have felled massive trees with these tools, but they could have pushed the forest back by trimming at the margins, clearing undergrowth and roots, lopping off branches, or even causing trees to weaken and die by cutting away bark in a ring right round the trunk. Whether people were using this new-found power in association with the planting of crops is not known. There was probably no need because many of the native plants are edible and could be harvested directly from the forest. It may only have been necessary to clear away vegetation around the individual wild food plants, giving them more space and light to grow. This type of environmental manipulation is still practised in New Guinea today.

At some stage people began to carve gardens out of the forest, and into their gardens they brought wild plants to grow. By careful tending and breeding they improved the yields and other useful characteristics of their crops. Some bananas, for example, are indigenous to the island and several varieties have been domesticated. Of the 200 or so species of plants that are eaten in New Guinea today about half are now grown in gardens or plantations. The others are still collected from the wild.

It is now believed by many archaeologists and biologists that agriculture here may have been started independently of agriculture in the rest of the world. That discovery has come as some surprise to archaeologists. The traditional view has been that Asian crops were exported during prehistoric times out into Melanesia and the Pacific islands, and this was how agriculture was begun in these places. It is now thought that the early settlers first learned to use and domesticate plants native to New Guinea and only later imported food species from elsewhere. The Asian crops that were introduced afterwards include several varieties of banana, yam and taro.

Some of the crops originally domesticated in New Guinea are now of worldwide importance. Breadfruit, for example, was first cultivated here. But most important of all was sugar. Sugar cane is now a major crop throughout the tropics and must surely be one of the most widespread and valuable living commodities on earth. It was the people of New Guinea who first took its wild ancestor from their forests and domesticated it. This took place many thousands of years ago, long before any written records. Biologists have traced the connection by studying the genetics of sugar cane across the world. They have compared the commercial strains with the wild and cultivated varieties in New Guinea and also with varieties from other locations where it might have originated. There is no doubt that it came first from New Guinea.

If the earliest human settlers on the island found a plentiful supply of familiar plants, the same cannot be said for the animals. Most of the larger ones would have been completely new to them. While sea levels were low the fauna of New Guinea and Australia freely intermingled, so that New Guinea supported a broad range of marsupials that people from South East Asia would never have seen.

While most of these were quite small compared with, say, the deer or rhinos of Asia, one or two would have made substantial meals. When people first arrived there were giant wallabies and huge herbivores called diprotodonts living here. The latter was a wombat, similar in size to a rhinoceros. Marsupial wolves called thylacines also prowled the forests and grasslands. There's no firm evidence that early settlers hunted these animals, but it's not an implausible suggestion. Later on, as people moved into the interior, they almost certainly had a severe impact on the populations of the large marsupials. By 10 000 years ago most of these were extinct.

Climate change, increasing human numbers, and more effective hunting methods all probably played a part. The same was true in Australia and indeed for large animals throughout the world. It was the same process that led to the extinction of mammoths and woolly rhinos in Europe and sabre-toothed cats, ground sloths and glyptodonts in the Americas.

The other New Guinea mammals were, as today, small in size, largely nocturnal and difficult to hunt. Furthermore, none was suitable for domestication. To catch these animals hunters would have needed to devise all kinds of ingenious traps, snares and other techniques. Over the years that is just what they have done, using an intimate knowledge of animal behaviour to evolve the best method of capture for each species. One of the techniques used by early man to flush out game was fire. Continuous burning of woodland and forest has now created man-made grasslands in both the highland and lowland regions of the island. The huge grassy expanse of the Markham Valley, just south of the Huon Peninsula, is entirely due to the burning activities of people. But in spite of the effectiveness of various methods the populations of edible animals have never been sufficient to provide major quantities of food. To this day, most traditional societies in New Guinea do not, indeed cannot, rely on great quantities of meat caught in the wild.

Destruction of animal and plant resources has almost certainly been going on in New Guinea, as elsewhere in the world, for as long as people have lived here. But this is a large island and the human population has always been small. And with only primitive technology that was all that was available until very recently, it is not surprising that much of the island remains wild.

New Guinea has had not just one wave of immigrants from Asia but at least two main invasions. The second came much later than the first, around 5000 years ago. It was part of a great wave of people who spread eastward right through the Pacific. Out on the remoter islands of the Pacific Ocean they eventually gave rise to the renowned Polynesian culture, but in New Guinea their culture merged in many ways with that of the original inhabitants.

These two stages of colonisation are still preserved in the languages used on the island. The people of New Guinea speak in about a thousand different tongues. That is about a fifth of the world's total among just five million people. It is surely the densest and most varied concentration of languages in the world. About three-quarters belong to the Papuan group. These are unique to New Guinea and many are mutually unintelligible. They are the result of the many years of island isolation experienced by the descendants of the early human settlers. The later group brought with them Austronesian languages, related to others in Asia and the Pacific. Today, groups speaking Austronesian and Papuan languages often live close together and may seem almost indistinguishable in the other elements of their lives.

The inhabitants of this whole area display a phenomenal diversity of cultures. Yet, on the other hand, they share several distinctive traditions that are now common throughout much of New Guinea, and which form the basis of Melanesian culture. These traditionally include: wealth based on pigs and shells; a diet based on a single, starchy staple such as sweet potato, taro or sago; small political units led by self-made 'big men'; and a belief in magic and sorcery. This Melanesian culture identifies the people of New Guinea and its offshore islands and clearly sets them apart from their neighbours either side, in South East Asia and the Pacific.

Although substantial elements of the original cultures and lifestyles remain they have been considerably eroded in this century by the intrusion and influence of outsiders. The most durable elements have definitely been those needed for survival, food being the most basic. The vast majority of the people on the island still live in a subsistence economy, relying on traditional staple crops and food that can be collected or hunted from the wild. The most common materials used for housing and fencing are still natural. Pigs are widely kept and exchanged as wealth, although other valuable objects such as shells have been almost entirely replaced by cash.

Ever since the colonial period the power of traditional leaders, or 'big men', has to some extent been constrained but they still hold considerable sway in rural communities. In Papua New Guinea the most successful of them have become provincial and national politicians, bringing a unique blend of Melanesian power play to government with a style that is theoretically based on the system in Westminster. The change from traditional, clan based, social controls to a system in which councils and governments are designed to wield more authority has been a painful one in this new democracy, with frequent outbursts of lawlessness a very obvious and violent symptom of the problems. In Irian Jaya the firm rule of the Indonesians seems to many of the local people more like a colonial occupation. Traditional power systems have been largely ignored and the province is controlled by the force of the combined police, military and intelligence services.

Missionaries have also had a profound effect on the culture of most of the New Guinea peoples. Papua New Guinea has the highest ratio of missionaries to population of any country in the world. The missions have provided schools and health services in remote areas but many have also insisted on the destruction of elements of local culture, ranging from traditional clothing to carvings and other works of art, and even to magnificent spirit houses that are often at the centre of village social life. However, on other occasions missionaries have actually protected local culture, and foremost among these are the Catholics. In the Asmat region of Irian Jaya the Catholic Crozier Mission has helped prevent the wholesale destruction of the local carving tradition. In the 1960s the Indonesian authorities began to destroy all elements of traditional custom in an effort to control the region, but the mission bought up many of the best carvings, opened a museum and then, when things relaxed, encouraged local carvers to resume their practice. Today they organise an annual competition and Asmat carving is now recognised as world class art and is no longer forbidden.

All this change on the island has introduced considerable confusion and a strange mixture of old and new. This was typified for me when I met a smart besuited man in a rural taxi. He was returning from his comfortable office job in Port Moresby not just to visit his relatives but to help them in a tribal war against their neighbours. Further evidence of his cross-cultural ties came when he revealed that he and all his village were Christians. I asked him how he could possibly attempt to kill his neighbours while remaining true to Christian teaching. 'Oh that's easy,' he said, 'we don't fight on a Sunday!'

Traditional Melanesian life was full of ceremony. Weddings, compensation payments, hunting, gardening and warfare – all needed rituals to impress rivals or to assuage evil spirits or the ghosts of ancestors. These ceremonies might involve elaborate costumes being worn, kundu drums or bamboo horns being played, and sometimes carvings being made. They would almost always require prolonged singing and dancing. Ceremonies for practical purposes such as compensations or weddings are still very much alive but those involving magic or spirits are now less commonly performed.

While we were filming at the village of Ayam in the Asmat region, it became clear to me that although these latter rituals are now rare they still hold considerable importance in the minds of people. We filmed a sago ceremony, which is undertaken before a tree is felled in order to placate the ancestor spirit who is believed to dwell in every sago tree. Although this is seldom done these days, perhaps less than once a year, the proceedings were performed with great care and considerable enthusiasm by dozens of men. Elders ensured that every aspect was carried out strictly according to tradition and the whole ceremony took over twenty-four hours to complete.

The island today is an intriguing mix of the old and new. Much is still remote and wild and the people little affected in their day-to-day lives by the outside world. Most have no roads to their villages and have to walk considerable distances to any town offering modern facilities or shops. In fact, the rugged nature of the island and the problems this poses for travel has probably been the greatest single factor in preventing the spread of the modern world reaching the interior. Even the capital city of Port Moresby, with its plush hotels, offices and embassies, still has no road connection to any other town in the country. The same is true of Jayapura, the provincial capital of Irian Jaya. For many people traditional travel, on foot or by canoe, is still the only feasible method of getting around. For long-distance journeys there's only one easy option: the rivers, the great highways to the interior.

Chapter Eight

HIGHWAYS

TO THE

INTERIOR

*T*wice a day there's an Air Niugini flight between the two towns of Wewak and Madang on the north coast of the island. On a fine day the view is superb. From the shoreline a vast, flat plain extends south for well over 100 kilometres before being dramatically terminated by the towering mountains of the central cordillera. Most of the land is covered by dense swamp forest with the occasional patch of open, watery grassland. By plane it takes only a quarter of an hour to cross; by land it's almost impenetrable.

Along the coastline the deep blue of the ocean is now and then stained the colour of milky coffee. Great plumes of this murky liquid extend for miles out to sea, the outflow of rivers and streams that stretch back deep into the thick and tangled vegetation, providing access right up to the base of the distant mountains. Even at the end of the twentieth century most human activity in these swamps, and in the many others that fringe the coast of the island, is restricted to the river margins. The rivers must have been even more important for the earliest human settlers, enabling them to move inland.

Much of the highland interior has a very high rainfall, around 3–4000 millimetres a year. In some locations it can be over 10 000 – that's over 30 feet of rain. Huge quantities of water spill down the mountain ramparts towards the sea, creating several large rivers on the way, the two largest of which are the Fly and the Sepik. The Fly is named after a British warship, HMS *Fly*, which navigated the waterway in 1845 to push back the known frontiers of the island for exploring Europeans.

Both rivers rise within a few kilometres of each other in the Star Mountains, on the border of Papua New Guinea and Irian Jaya. The Fly plunges south towards the Gulf of Papua and travels 1200 kilometres before reaching the sea, making it the longest river on the island. In terms of the volume of water it discharges, about 13 000 cubic metres every second, it is one of the most powerful rivers in the world. It ends in a vast delta system of shifting islands and shallow channels, with a mouth over 80 kilometres wide.

To the north the Sepik tumbles sharply down the mountain slopes onto a vast floodplain. It does not flow quite as far as the Fly, only 1100 kilometres, or pick up quite as much water, but in many other ways it can claim to be the greatest and most interesting river system in New Guinea. Its catchment area, with literally hundreds of large and small tributaries, is larger than that of the Fly. It covers a huge area of land, nearly 80 000 square kilometres in all, and runs through almost every type of environment on the island. Remarkably, the Sepik is less than 6000 years old. The creation of such a large river system in such a short period of time has had dramatic consequences for the people, plants and animals of the Sepik Basin.

Originally the Sepik Basin, along with the adjacent but smaller Ramu River, was filled with salt water. It was a great inland sea, over 200 metres deep and extending 250 kilometres into the interior, right up to the foothills of the central mountains. Six thousand years ago the last ice age had finally ended and much of the waters held in glaciers had melted. Sea levels around the world had stabilised, but torrential tropical rainfall continued to erode at the mountains of the interior. Rivers cut into the land and carried away heavy loads of sediment. The mountains were literally moved, as billions of tiny particles, towards the sea. As the short river that would eventually become the Sepik reached the coast it lost its power and dumped the sediment from the mountains on the floor of the inland sea. Slowly it filled and the coastline was pushed further to the north. By about 1000 years ago the river had created a floodplain extending all the way to the northern edge of the island. The ocean is very deep at this point and the sediment flowing from the river mouth was swept far away on the currents.

The changing shoreline and recent birth of this river have created an enormous diversity of human culture in this one area: about 200 languages are spoken in this corner of the island alone. As the river system grew and evolved it encouraged large-scale migration. At the same time the ever changing course of the waterways split up the landscape again and again, encouraging the break-up of human populations. Even to this day the peoples of the Sepik are generally not organised into large tribes: their society remains ordered at the village level. As the rivers wandered over the floodplain cutting new channels, the villages have had to move with them. Today, people on one bank of a small tributary may well speak a different language from their neighbours opposite, but yet may share a common tongue with villagers 20 kilometres downstream.

The effect of this extensive new river system on aquatic life has been quite different. The diversity of freshwater fish found here must be one of the lowest for any comparably sized river in the world, because they simply have not had time to evolve. The high mountain barriers to the south have prevented fish from infiltrating the Sepik from the other side of the island. And to the north lies only deep ocean, and that is where they have had to swim in from. Of the handful of fish species that today inhabit the Sepik and its tributaries, all are either recently evolved from marine species or are actually marine fish that have been able to migrate into and survive in freshwater.

This means that fishing is severely limited in scope, and protein deficiency has always been a real problem. Over the past few decades foreign fish such as tilapia and carp have been deliberately introduced. Before then gudgeons, tarpon and a few species of rather tasteless catfish made up the bulk of the catch. There are no native species able to exploit fully the vast areas of seasonally flooded plains. The Sepik floodplain produces only a tenth the quantity of fish a similarly sized area in Africa would provide.

Occasionally, however, sharks have been hooked or trapped. They have been found swimming far upriver, even in shallow lakes. Presumably the hunting is good, with no competition from the usual freshwater predators such as pike or perch. They are well equipped to seek out prey in these murky waters where visibility is often no more than a few centimetres. Using a powerful sense of smell and, during the final approach, the ability to detect the tiny electrical impulses emitted by the muscles of the prey, a shark can home in on and attack its victim without ever needing to see it.

Sharks are not the only unusual fish that occasionally find their way into the cooking pot. Sawfish are related to sharks but look and behave quite differently. They are very odd-looking fish, flattened like a ray, but with a long, thin snout extending perhaps a metre in front of the mouth, and armed on either side with sharp, horizontally pointing teeth. They lurk around on the bottom using the saw to stir up crustaceans and molluscs which they capture and crush with teeth especially flattened for just this purpose. Some biologists claim that the fish can use its saw to slash from side to side and impale its prey. Even if true this does not sound like a very efficient way of catching a meal.

They breed quite happily in freshwater even though they are really marine animals. The offspring receive maximum protection before birth; they are not expelled as vulnerable eggs but as well-developed youngsters. In some parts of New Guinea sawfish even live in land-locked bodies of water with no access to the sea. Until recently they were found in Sentani Lake near Jayapura, the capital of Irian Jaya, but they now seem to have been wiped out from this particular spot, possibly because of overfishing.

Some of the most spectacular marine creatures to have used the rivers as highways to the interior are the large saltwater crocodiles. These have remained almost unchanged since the age of the dinosaurs. Big males may grow to over 6 metres in length and have been known to hunt and kill dogs, domestic pigs, even people. They are the largest crocodiles on earth. Salties, as they are commonly called, have been found over 1000 kilometres upriver in swift-flowing rocky streams, but they are far more common down in the lakes and swamps of the floodplain. That they should travel so far inland is surprising because they are the most marine of all the world's crocodiles. They have been spotted hundreds of kilometres away from land, far out in the Pacific Ocean.

Salties are also amongst the most aquatic of all crocodiles, spending most of their time in the water except when they need to come ashore to lay eggs. It's rare to see them basking on a river bank like the Nile crocodiles in Africa; they prefer to bask in the water, finding a calm and shallow patch of stream or lakeside in which to rest and warm their massive bodies. This behaviour may be natural but it might also be caused by man.

Salties live throughout the tropics but have been hunted for their valuable skins and are now rare and endangered across most of their range. New Guinea is one of their last strongholds, although here too hunting has been heavy. These reptiles are so shy that on the Sepik, and most other rivers, it's unusual to see a crocodile during daylight hours. The best time to observe them is at night. The easiest way is in a quiet canoe, and armed with a powerful torch. In places where they are common the canoe will become surrounded by pairs of bright, shining eyes. With the torch focused on an animal's face to dazzle it, they can be approached quite closely, a technique also used very successfully by the hunters.

Throughout the Sepik region young children play and swim in the rivers, streams and lakes around their villages. They do this in apparent safety. It seems that the crocodiles have, in the main, learnt to avoid crowds of people and the attendant risk of death. But a person swimming alone and away from such regular bathing spots is certainly at risk. These animals are at the head of the Sepik food-chain and will not pass up an opportunity for an easy meal. They have obviously been successful because they have barely changed in two hundred million years of evolution. As well as the saltwater crocodile there is another species that also inhabits these waters. The New Guinea crocodile is considerably smaller than the saltie and is restricted to freshwater habitats on this island and parts of neighbouring Indonesia.

In Papua New Guinea the government, private companies and local villagers have teamed up to try and save both species by harvesting them in a sustainable way. If this is successful the income they provide will be an incentive for local people to protect and value them as a living resource. In the past it has generally been the largest crocodiles that have been hunted because they have the biggest, most valuable skins. But they are also the most valuable to the breeding population, and a reduction in their numbers causes a decline in the overall population. The key to sustainable crocodile harvesting is to collect eggs or youngsters. These can then be raised until the crocodiles are sufficiently large to be killed for their skins. In this way the large breeding animals are left alone and can easily lay another replacement clutch of eggs later on.

But to get started at all with a project such as this the eggs have to be collected first, and mother crocodiles do not make that easy. Along the banks of the Sepik, and especially in the myriad shallow lakes of the floodplain, mats of vegetation float on the water's surface. These are mosaics of several different kinds of plant that can survive without being permanently anchored to land. Some mats are low, with only grasses and a few small bushes; others have high forests of sago and other trees. As far as human beings are concerned their most distinctive feature is that they are almost impossible to walk on. Apart from the tangle of vegetation, the floor of fallen debris on which they sit is usually soft and will not reliably support the weight of a person. It is in just such places, of course, that female crocodiles choose to build their nests. The mats are conveniently close to the water, yet because they float there is no risk of flooding. Combine those advantages with the inaccessibility of this type of habitat and it becomes a perfect breeding location. To attempt to collect eggs in such a place, in the knowledge that there's almost certainly a large and powerful mother crocodile lurking nearby waiting for an opportunity to rush out and protect her clutch, might seem foolhardy. But people do it, albeit sometimes with the aid of modern technology.

Every March, at the end of the rainy season when the crocodiles are breeding, a helicopter with specialist biologists arrives in the Sepik Basin. They enlist the help of local men who know the area well and, just as importantly, know who owns the land that each nest is on. The helicopter can drop a person right on top of the nests to make a hurried collection and a swift getaway before the mother realises what is happening. The villagers who own each nest site are paid for the eggs. These are then taken off to a crocodile farm to be hatched, raised, and then killed for their skins. This may seem a harsh fate but the Sepik is a harsh place to live. An income such as that which the crocodiles provide can be a vital economic incentive, encouraging people to protect their lands and the crocodiles and other animals that inhabit them.

The Sepik people have the greatest respect for crocodiles. Indeed in one myth it is the crocodile who created the earth and sky from the the mists that hang above the water. Many villages still include the crocodile in their daily lives and ritual ceremonies. The most visible evidence of this are the carved prows of everyday canoes. In some villages even the tiniest canoes have crocodile heads hewn out of the wood at their bows. But more astonishing to the western eye is the skin carving of men's bodies and the ritual behind this practice.

Throughout New Guinea young boys have traditionally undergone initiation rites. The villages on the Sepik are no different and in many tribes here the crocodile has a special place in the ceremonies. Before young boys are ready to be initiated into the adult world they are separated from general society for several weeks or months. They spend their time in the village spirit house or Haus Tamboran. Until missionaries arrived, and later the Japanese during the Second World War, every village had a spirit house. Those that have survived being burnt down by zealous Christians or military overlords are still in use. Many are spectacular structures, towering over the landscape, with a steeply pitched roof rising about as high as that of an English village church.

After their period of isolation, and having passed through the rituals inside the spirit house, the boys emerge as men. They are changed not only in mind but in body too. Up their arms, over their shoulders, and down their backs and legs the youths bear a series of apparently horrific scars. These scars are arranged in neat rows and represent the teeth marks of a crocodile. The story that each young man tells is that he was swallowed by one of these great reptiles and was then reborn as a crocodile-man, possessing all the strength of the beast that had eaten him alive. The young boys had not been swallowed by a crocodile, but they did undergo an experience almost as painful.

The scars were made when one of the older men in the village made a series of cuts on the boys' skin. In the past this would have been done with a piece of sharp bamboo, but now a razor-blade is a more likely tool. The whole painful process takes several hours and at the end of it the bleeding wounds are rubbed with oil. This ensures that the scars which develop will be large and prominent. It also helps cleanse the cuts.

With the incursion of the modern world into their society everyone now knows that the crocodile story is only a myth, but boys still bravely submit to this punishing rite of passage. In Sepik villages young men proudly display their crocodile cuts and charge tourists for photographing their bodies.

Both crocodiles and people live in a constantly changing world. This is true not only of the recent changes brought about by contact with the modern world but also because of the very nature of the place in which they live. Their world has always been on the move; the river and its path are never still. The main channel drops less than 50 metres in its final 1000 kilometres to the sea. Because of this gentle gradient it meanders sluggishly across a broad floodplain. As the years pass the bends move across the land by cutting into their outer banks and depositing silt on their inner ones. Through the decades these meanders cross and recross each other, cutting off ox-bow lakes on the one hand and creating totally new channels on the other. New land is created in one place while village sites are swept away in another, and houses and gardens have to be moved every few years.

The mats of plants floating on the many lakes of the floodplain are blown about by the wind and change the shape of the shoreline and the configuration of open water in a matter of hours. Some form islands that are spun round and round until they are perfectly circular in shape. Circles of all sizes pile up together like a group of giant pennies on a shove-halfpenny board.

The Blackwater Lakes, just south of the middle Sepik, are just such a shifting, watery world. Their name comes from the dark peaty water that flows through them on its way from the mountains to the Kosameri River and then to the Sepik itself. They can be entered by canoe in the morning, and by the afternoon you can be hopelessly lost trying to weave through a maze of channels that bears only a partial resemblance to those that were there only a few hours before. Walking over what looks like dry land is impossible. The grassy banks may seem thick and solid but they are merely a light veneer of matted vegetation covering the dark waters below. The grass itself is savage. Each blade is razor-sharp. It tears and slashes at the bare skin of any unprotected leg or arm that passes through it.

During the dry season, between May and September, water levels fall and the shoreline changes yet again. Where once it was possible to paddle right up to the small villages around the lakes they now stand perhaps half a kilometre from open water. The drying mud on the edge of the lakes bursts into a riot of colour before it finally cakes hard and cracks. Among the grass bloom huge pink water lilies, their stems pushing the flowers almost a metre above the mud on which their large floating leaves lie. With a final effort they suck water from beneath the surface of the soil and spread their bright pink petals to reveal hearts of pretty yellow stamens. Hundreds may stand together in this way, a dazzling spectacle in the monotonous sea of grass.

For the birds too, the drying out is a time of change. Many fish and frogs that were once able to move freely beneath the floating vegetation become trapped in shrinking pools. Dozens of egrets and pied herons congregate in each tiny patch of water to take advantage of this potential feast. They stand motionless, waiting for a tell-tale ripple to give their prey away. The egrets are a glossy white, but the pied herons resemble nothing so closely as a Victorian bank clerk standing rather rigidly, with long black tail coat and a starched white shirt. They also have a charming little tuft of black feathers hanging from the top of their head.

During the dry season travel on the rivers and lakes is rather monotonous. Not only are the banks brown and caked with mud, the water is so low that it's also impossible to see over the tops of them from a canoe. In the wet season the floods rise so high that in many places the banks disappear completely and the view stretches almost to the horizon.

With frequent flooding, ordinary crops are almost impossible to grow. It's not just a matter of the river water gently topping the banks; it can rise over 7 metres during the wet season. People in the Sepik region therefore rely on a very special crop to provide them with the bulk of their vegetable intake – sago.

Sago is a palm that grows naturally throughout the swamplands, but over the millennia people have learnt how to encourage it to grow in specific and convenient locations. They have also learnt how to eat it. This is not easy because the leaves are inedible and the only part of nutritional value lies in the trunk and requires special processing.

The tree takes about fifteen years to mature and needs to be harvested just before it flowers, which it does only once in its life. During its long period of growth the sago stores up a great supply of starch. If the plant is left alone it will use this energy store to produce a massive spike of flowers. It then dies and is of no use. The whole tree must be cut down before this and dragged either to the village or to a convenient clearing on a river bank. The bark is split and the pith inside is beaten into small fragments and then washed with river water. As the water flows through the pith it dissolves the starch within it and this is then allowed to settle out as a thick gooey mess. Such apparently unpromising material is the basis of much Sepik cuisine.

Before it can be cooked the sago starch has to be dried in the sun to create a powder not unlike flour in appearance. Only after all this effort can the cooking begin. There are two main recipes for sago and neither is very sophisticated. One is for sago pancakes, the other for sago pudding. The first is the easiest. A shallow metal bowl is heated over a small fire and the sago powder is simply poured in. It immediately hardens into a pancake, which is flattened and rolled with half a coconut shell before being flipped over to brown the other side. The end result is a thick pancake with a crisp exterior and a soft chewy inside. To most western palates it's rather bland but to the people of the Sepik it's a staple food and can be taken anywhere – on hunting, fishing or shopping expeditions.

Sago pudding, on the other hand, is rather messy. It's made by mixing the powder with boiling water. At first nothing happens, then, a few seconds later, the solution suddenly turns into a thick, pinkish, gelatinous lump. Eaten with fish and edible leaves, it is perhaps the equivalent of mashed potatoes in a European diet. Such a diet of fish and sago is filling but not totally nutritious, but it's just about the only way to make a living off the land in this area where neither land nor water are permanent fixtures.

People have to rely on the sago tree for more than just food: its leaves are used as roofing material; young shoots are split and the fibres made into grass skirts, and they can also be spun into long lengths of string; sago thorns come in handy as needles; the outside of the leaf stems are woven into fish traps; and the bark is split and flattened into floorboards, as well as being made into canoe bailers, fashioned into storage jars, and even burnt to extract the salt that's held inside.

For major building materials, especially the great logs required for the main frames of their houses, people may have to travel many kilometres to find suitable trees. These grow only on slightly higher and drier patches of ground. All the houses in the region are built on stilts, partly to prevent flooding, and partly to try and raise the sleeping area above the flight paths of mosquitoes. These insects carry malaria, which, in the swamps of the Sepik floodplain, is a major killer, especially of young children. In the distant past it would have been an even more dangerous environment in which to live because of frequent tribal warfare and head-hunting raids.

In spite of all the hardships the inhabitants of the area are accomplished artists. Sepik sculpture and painting is internationally famous. Masks, spirit figures, painted story boards, carved cult hooks and decorated spirit houses are part of a rich and spectacular culture. The art, and the way in which it is used in ceremony and rites, reflect the many fears and hopes of people who have always lived in a dangerous and changing world over which they have traditionally had little control. The art is partly a tool to help people gain some power over those threatening natural forces. Seen in that light, it's perhaps not surprising that such a rich culture has thrived in one of the most difficult and inhospitable swamps on earth.

Most of the land on the Sepik floodplain is entirely flat, but inland, at its edge, low hills begin to rise. From these the extent of the swamps can be seen. There is perhaps one place, not far from the Blackwater Lakes as the egret flies, that provides an unparalleled view. It's the verandah of a lodge called Karawari, set on a ridge just above the river of the same name.

Because the forest has been cleared to make way for the lodge the view towards the Sepik River is unobscured. It's magnificent. A great swamp of sago and other trees stretches to the north. In the middle distance lie the glinting waters of the Blackwater Lakes. Beside them stands an isolated hill, Murder Mountain, so named because of the Australian soldiers executed there by the Japanese in the Second World War. In the distance the shadows of the Hunstein Range sit on the horizon. To the south and west lie the foothills of the central cordillera, beginning their climb towards summits at over 4000 metres.

As the dry season comes to a close towering thunderstorms march across this view. The panorama is so broad that while the sun may be setting over the distant mountains, in another direction a great, grey wall of torrential rain might be falling well within view. With forks of lightning stabbing at yet another part of the plain, the scene can be almost unreal, as if from an imaginary world.

Just a little further up the Karawari River a small tributary leads off towards another magical world, right at the far southern limits of the Sepik floodplain. The tributary is called the Arafundi. Travelling upstream at sunrise in a small canoe is the best way to make the journey. At this time of day wisps of mist hang just above the water and at the right time of year thousands of dainty, white lace-winged insects dance on the still surface of the stream. A melodious dawn chorus echoes from the surrounding forest. Clusters of glorious red flowers hang from creepers at the water's edge. Officially they are called D'Albertis creeper, but their common name is far more expressive – flame of the forest.

After perhaps an hour of travel a narrow breach suddenly appears in the right-hand river bank. If it has been raining heavily water gushes through in a torrent. The stream bubbles along a passage lined with reeds that hang out so far they meet in the middle. Passing through this claustrophobic little channel you suddenly emerge in light – a lake stretches away into the distance. On an overcast day the sky, the water and the mist blend in such a way that it's impossible to tell where one ends and the other begins. After the rushing water of the Arafundi this world seems strangely silent. Only the distant call of a tern or whistling kite disturbs the stillness. These are the Jimas Lakes.

As the sun rises higher and burns away the fog green mountains appear on the horizon. These are the last lakes on the floodplain. Beyond, the streams that feed the lakes, and eventually the great Sepik River itself, disappear steeply up into the hills towards their source. The first lake is only one of three, each quite distinctive though linked to the rest. They are joined by narrow channels that wind between floating mats of razor grass.

The first lake is covered in hundreds of pretty white and yellow water lilies. They are dotted among dense rafts of floating plants. The lilies and other vegetation provide places to feed and breed for several types of bird. Most immediately conspicuous are the comb-crested jacanas, or lily trotters as they are commonly known. These are small black birds with long legs and enormous feet that allow them to walk on lily pads and other floating plants. At times the lily trotters seem to be walking on the water itself. Complementing their long legs are long necks, with a delicate splash of cream on the throat. On top of their head, and the reason for their name, they carry a bright pink swelling, the comb. This is important in sexual attraction and display.

The jacanas are fun to watch as they strut around in search of aquatic insects and other titbits hidden among the plants. But keep watching and they are more fascinating still. Each male controls a territory, a portion of the lake. If another male wanders just a little too close the territory holder stands on tiptoe, stretches his neck high, stares at the intruder and calls in a threatening voice. If this does not work he sets off with wings audibly whirring to drive off the rival. After a short aerial chase, which invariably seems to succeed, the resident returns to continue feeding. By observing the birds for some time it's possible to work out the size of each male's territory, about a hectare.

Females fly over the territories of several males and seem to initiate courtship. Once copulation is complete it's the male who begins nest building near the site where the actual mating took place. Later the female returns and lays eggs in his nest. In many species of jacana the female travels from male to male depositing eggs in their nests and leaving them to incubate the clutch. The female comb-crested jacana seems to be the exception. She usually breeds with only one male and helps rear the young. Because they feed, mate and nest in very short, floating vegetation they are easily observed from a boat. After a short while they will ignore an observer and wander quite calmly to within almost an arm's length or so.

The other water birds will come close too. Few are as charming as the white pygmy geese. They are actually ducks but at first sight look like miniature geese. They travel in pairs on the Jimas Lakes. The male is a creamy white and his mate a dull brown. They follow each other about, nibbling around the flowers and pads of the lilies.

Whistling ducks, on the other hand, upend themselves to feed underwater on the stalks of lilies and other plants.

Passing from the first lake to either of the second two takes you through narrow channels with old wooden stumps and branches poking out of the water. These provide convenient resting places for terns and cormorants. Cormorants fish in large flocks, up to 100 strong. They work together, driving shoals of fish into shallow water near the banks, where they can corner them for eating.

It is also at this point that the tropical rainforest meets the water. It rises from the lakes over a series of steep hills to the mountains beyond. A vantage point out on the water provides a fantastic view of the canopy. The lakes permit an unobstructed view to the hillside, something rarely possible from inside the forest itself. The crowns of the trees are a riot of colour, not only different shades of green, but yellows, oranges and reds. Some trees stick out above the general level, but wherever they do so they are covered in a thick coat of climbing plants. The impression the hillside presents is of a great and impenetrable living wall.

This is just about as far as the easy journey goes. The rivers beyond are not smooth and gentle; they are fast-flowing streams, blocked by rapids and waterfalls. The only way forward is by foot, on narrow tracks and trails through thick jungle into the hills and mountains beyond.

Chapter Nine

HIDDEN VALLEYS

*F*rom most vantage points on the coast of New Guinea the overwhelming view of the interior is one of towering, cloud-capped mountains. In some spots, like the Huon Peninsula on the north-east of the island, they rise abruptly and dramatically from the sea. Further along that northern coast the great swamps of the Ramu and Sepik rivers intervene between the shoreline and the slopes. But wherever a journey is made into the interior, formidable walls of rock eventually bar the way. They rise spectacularly towards the sky, with thick vegetation clinging to their sides and shining waterfalls cascading from their distant summits.

Ever since the first European explorers sailed by in the early sixteenth century it had been assumed that the centre of the island, beyond these natural barriers, was a colossal mass of impenetrable mountains incapable of supporting any human life. Four hundred years later that was still the view of the colonial authorities who ruled New Guinea at the turn of the century. Such an inhospitable and apparently valueless interior was not even considered worth the trouble and danger of exploring. So it was, that as late as the 1920s no outsiders had penetrated most of the hinterland. It was one of the last great unknown areas of the globe. But a gold rush changed all that.

Ever since the Portuguese discovered the island in 1526 rumours had persisted that fabulous quantities of gold lay within its hills. The Spanish conquistador Cortez sent ships to explore it in 1527, after failing to find his El Dorado in Mexico. They found only a few traces of gold but, nevertheless, named it 'Isla del Oro'. In 1606 Luis Vaez de Torres, a Portuguese adventurer working for the King of Spain, reported that there was certainly gold to be found in the mountains of New Guinea because they were so similar in appearance to the gold bearing hills of Peru. Similar rumours continued to circulate through the successive centuries, but, with such a hostile land to penetrate and little proof to back up these claims, nobody bothered to look seriously until the late nineteenth century. Even then only a few small and relatively insignificant strikes were unearthed – until 1926.

In that year huge quantities of gold were discovered in a small tributary of the Bulolo River at an altitude of about 1000 metres above sea level. It was called Edie Creek. As news reached Australia of miners staggering out of the jungle with sackfuls of gold on their backs, hundreds of hopeful prospectors set sail for the shores of New Guinea. Although Edie Creek was less than 60 kilometres from the coast, it took the men over a week of tough walking over steep, slippery, forested ridges to reach the site of the mine. The difficult terrain, a sapping tropical climate, malaria and many other nasty diseases soon made it clear to the new arrivals why much of New Guinea remained unexplored.

But with positive proof of gold in the hills the opening up of the highland interior became almost inevitable. The man who was to pioneer that in a big way was Michael Leahy, a prospector at Edie Creek, who had almost had a fortune within reach but then lost it. Due to a series of mishaps and illness he finished the gold rush with little money but with a burning desire to find his own El Dorado. On the morning of 26 May 1930 he set out from a mission post at the border of known territory on a prospecting expedition with colleague Michael Dwyer and a group of native porters.

After a hard day's march the expedition had managed to climb several lines of heavily forested ridges but had failed to find a suitable place to camp for the night. As the sun was setting they came over the crest of one more hill and suddenly before them lay a completely unexpected sight. Instead of further mountains stretching off into the distance, as they had assumed there would be, the men saw open grassy slopes. In fact they had stumbled across a hidden highland valley. As night fell they were in for an even more astonishing surprise; the lights of many fires began to twinkle on the walls of the valley around them. It was inhabited. Expecting attack before daybreak, they spent a restless night, heavily armed and ready to fight. But morning dawned uneventfully and before long they made contact with the previously unknown human population, people who had never before set eyes on white men.

The locals were all well armed and carrying bows and arrows. But far from attacking the Australians and their porters the people gazed at them in awe, shock and, in the case of many, sheer terror. The appearance of fair-skinned men in their land was an eventuality for which their isolated life, enclosed within the confines of steep mountain walls, had given them little preparation. To them there seemed only one explanation for this event. It was an explanation that took firm hold wherever the strangers went. They were quite simply thought to be mythological characters, most probably the ghosts of ancestors returning from the dead. Believing them to be their long departed relatives, it was perhaps not surprising that the local people in no way harmed or attacked the white men.

This was to be only the first of many such contacts over the next few years, because what Leahy and Dwyer had inadvertently stumbled on here was just part of the greatest concentration of people on the whole island. The events that followed during the 1930s were the last great discoveries of previously unknown human populations to be made anywhere on earth. Later it transpired that Lutheran missionaries had in fact spied these people a few years earlier but had kept quiet, wanting to spare them the complications of contact with the outside world. But with gold now the driving force it was only a matter of time before the full impact of the twentieth century would hit these isolated mountain people and their hidden valleys. It was not long, for example, before the people learnt something of the white man's lethal power. As their curiosity value wore off on second and third visits explorers were attacked and attempts were made to steal their property. Inevitably, highlanders were killed in a hail of bullets.

Throughout the 1930s more and more highland valleys and their human inhabitants were discovered. The known population grew to several hundred thousand. The mountains that everyone had assumed peaked in the centre of the island were a series of ranges separated by broad flat valleys at altitudes of around 1200 to 1800 metres. Most of the valleys were originally steep-sided but at some time in the past landslides, caused by volcanic activity, had blocked the rivers that flowed through them. These backed up into lakes, and sediment settled out on the bottom. Eventually the rivers carved other routes out of the valleys and left them dry once more. But so much alluvium had been laid down that their floors had now become relatively flat, and very fertile too, ideal for human settlement and agriculture. When the white men found them most were full of people.

The rugged terrain that had originally discouraged explorers from venturing inland was not the only reason that these people had remained unknown to the outside world. As the prospectors moved from one group of homesteads to the next the crowds that were following them would drop back and act in alarm at the apparent intentions of the strangers to continue their journey. It was obvious that the people regarded their neighbours as vicious enemies who would immediately slay the newcomers if they ventured into their territory. Time and again, in valley after valley, this was repeated. It soon became clear that the population was organised into small clans and that each clan was continually in a state of tension, if not open warfare, with its neighbours.

In such a situation it was impossible for anyone to travel safely more than a few kilometres from their place of birth. The highlanders knew of no world other than that of their immediate surroundings. Exploratory missions further afield were out of the question. Even a flow of news from clan to clan was difficult because there was no common language. Just about the only obvious influence to have reached these mountain valleys was the presence of certain goods traded up from the coast through numerous hands. Sea shells, for example, were used as valuable jewellery or currency.

Although these highlanders had never seen a wheel, used no beasts of burden, and were, in effect, still living in the stone age, they were far from primitive. As exploration and study over the ensuing decades revealed, these people had evolved a range of culture that was complex and truly remarkable. And without the aid of metal tools they had developed ways of using their land to grow crops that were rooted in an ancient history and yet had a modern sophistication to rival agricultural practices anywhere else in the world.

One of the most astonishing discoveries was not made by gold prospectors in Papua New Guinea but by a joint Dutch and American scientific expedition into the centre of Irian Jaya in 1938. It was already known that a great valley lay inland, but not until the American, Richard Archbold, flew over the Grand Baliem Valley in a giant seaplane in that year was the full extent of this hidden world revealed. Below him was a huge plain, perhaps 70 kilometres long by 15 wide, covered in neat geometric gardens and drainage ditches. The valley walls were covered in stone terraces, and in among the gardens and houses stood tall watchtowers. A whole civilisation of 50 000 people, living in isolation in the largest highland valley of all, had remained hidden to outside view until Archbold arrived in 1938. Over the following fourteen months tonnes of food and other supplies and dozens of men were flown in to explore this unknown world.

It was not an accident that these highland valleys turned out to support the greatest population densities on the island. The conditions were well suited for human settlement, and there is evidence of human occupation going back 26 000 years. At that time the climate would have been much colder because the world was still in the grip of the ice ages. But from about 10 000 years ago, when the ice had receded up the mountains, forests of oak, southern beech and pine would have clothed these valleys and their walls. The climate here was cooler, drier and generally more pleasant than in the hot and steamy lowlands. It was also far healthier because there was no malaria.

Judging by the range of food and other products still collected from wild plants, there must have been a rich and varied resource base for early arrivals to exploit. Edible plants are common: *Pandanus* trees provide nuts and oils and the forests are full of dozens of varieties of fruiting vine. Breadfruit grows here naturally as do edible fungi, ferns, tubers and greens. Dyes, salts, cosmetics, poisons and medicines are all to be found among the plants of the region.

And clothing, tools, houses, musical instruments, weapons, ornaments, fences, baskets and rope can all be fashioned from bush materials, and continue to be constructed from them to this day.

The Huli of Papua New Guinea were one of the last of the major highland tribes to be contacted, and in many ways they maintain a more traditional life than most. They still rely on the surrounding bush for many of their requirements. Their houses are mostly still built from thatched leaves and kunai grass. They stand low so the fire inside stands a chance of keeping the dwelling warm during the cool highland nights. While sitting one evening in a men's house I saw how many objects in everyday use are still made from natural products. Each man wore a traditional bark belt to which a twine apron was attached at the front and *Cordyline* leaves, or arse grass as it's known locally, at the back. At his waist every man carried a dagger cum digging stick fashioned from the thigh bone of a cassowary. While one man twisted rope from vegetable fibres, another whittled arrows from freshly cut blackpalm wood. A bamboo tube made an excellent pipe in which some of the men smoked local tobacco, while smaller sections were being gently played as pan pipes. Almost everything in the building, except for a crate of South Pacific beer, was made of local materials. One recent estimate suggests that over 600 plants throughout the highlands are used in some way or another.

But these highlanders are in no way hunter-gatherers. Around 10 000 years ago they began to develop agriculture. The earliest archaeological evidence unearthed so far is at a location called Kuk in the Western Highlands province of Papua New Guinea. It dates back to 9000 years ago and consists of an artificial canal, basins, pits and stakeholes, as well as clues in the soil that suggest the area had been cleared of forest. To put this in perspective, Europe was only just emerging from the last ice age at this time and hunter-gatherers were still chasing mammoths as a source of food. Even in the fertile crescent of the Middle East, to where the origins of modern cereal growing can be traced, the cultivation of grain crops had barely begun. So it seems likely that agriculture in New Guinea may have arisen independently and as early in history as anywhere in the world.

The soils in the highlands are often fertile enough to support crops for several years in succession before they need to be left fallow, and the lowish temperatures mean that weeds do not grow as profusely as in the lowlands. These conditions, combined with plentiful tropical sun and rain, are ideal for gardening. At first local plants were probably domesticated and brought into cultivation – plants such as banana, sugar cane, pitpit, beans and a variety of greens. But taro and yams soon followed, probably imported from South East Asia and traded up from the coast. But when these valleys were opened up this century it was none of these plants that provided the staple diet, but a crop from far away South America.

The sweet potato was probably introduced into Asia several hundred years ago by Europeans travelling from their colonies in the Americas. From there it found its way to New Guinea. The highlands were not directly linked to the coast by formal trade routes so the sweet potato probably spread slowly, over many years, from village to village, until eventually it reached the mountain valleys. Once it arrived here it became by far the most important crop. It generally provides somewhere between 70 per cent and 90 per cent of the daily calorie intake. But that's not to say that all highland gardens are the same or contain the same types of sweet potato. There are dozens of varieties each with its own recognised properties of growth, shape and flavour. The highlanders have never been slow to adopt new ideas and improvements, and even today are continually introducing new crops and new varieties of old ones into their gardens.

Flying over the highlands, the unique nature of the agriculture is clear from the pattern of neatly laid out gardens. The most conspicuous features of all are the mounds built for sweet potato growing. They dot the landscape in regimented rows. Each mound is a couple of metres in diameter and neatly spaced from the next. The soil in between is carefully cleared. Such mounds are particularly pronounced in the Southern Highlands province of Papua New Guinea.

The mounds are a unique and highly successful way of growing sweet potatoes. The tilled soil is well aerated and conducive to the growth of the cuttings buried in it. The rotting vegetation inside the mound gently composts and raises the soil temperature, while the mound itself causes cold air and water to sink and spill away.

In this way the crop is protected from flooding and from the occasional frosts that descend on these valleys.

In some areas large swamps have been drained for growing sweet potatoes. The Baliem Valley in Irian Jaya would once have been regularly waterlogged but the Dani gardeners have constructed a complex network of drainage ditches and canals to control water levels. These must be many hundreds of years old. The ditches not only serve as drains but also connect with the local streams, and during dry periods the flow of water can be reversed to irrigate the gardens. They are also used as mulching beds. Topsoil washes into them and, as the sweet potato vines are pruned or the mounds weeded, all the detritus is thrown into a nearby ditch where it decomposes and creates a rich organic mulch. When the ground is being reworked for a planting this is all scooped up and thrown onto the new mounds to fertilise the soil. By combining this system with short fallow periods between harvesting and replanting the soil is kept permanently productive.

Because sweet potatoes can grow higher than the other crops, often up to 2000 metres and occasionally in Irian Jaya to almost 3000 metres, and are easy to produce in vast quantities, their introduction several hundred years ago almost certainly led to an expansion of the human population in the highlands. But it also led to more subtle changes in culture. Because large amounts of food could be produced there was the question of what to do with any surplus. Sweet potato cannot be stored for later use and in any case there was no need. Individuals could just wander out into their gardens each day and gather plenty to eat. The solution was to store the surplus in the bodies of pigs.

Pigs are not native to New Guinea but were introduced at least 6000 years ago. Today they have a central role in highland society. Most of the gardening is undertaken by women and to them too falls the responsibility of pig husbandry. Each day they take the animals to the gardens and tether them close by. If they are constructing new sweet potato mounds the women allow the pigs to root around in the ground they are about to prepare. In this way the pigs get to feed off any remaining sweet potato tubers while helping the women by churning the soil.

In the evening the pigs accompany the women back to their

homes. Some spend the night in specially built sties; others sleep in the same huts as the women and their children. While food is prepared for the evening meal the animals are thrown scraps and even whole sweet potato tubers. The pigs often have names and are treated as part of the family, being stroked, fondled, and gently spoken to as the children prepare for bed. By tickling their udders and imitating the action of a suckling piglet females can be encouraged to lie down quietly on their side to be gently de-ticked. But these are neither pets nor regular food animals. They are being raised for very particular ceremonial reasons.

We witnessed one of these events near the town of Tari. We had stopped our truck on the side of a small dirt track when, in the distance, we heard the chanting of a large crowd of people. It drew nearer and nearer along the road and then all of a sudden around the corner came a charging mass of fully armed warriors. Each wielded bow and arrows and some carried large knives and axes as well. Many had long bamboo sticks through holes in their noses and all had painted faces – some yellow, others black, a few bright red. On their backs hung decorative hornbill beaks. Most bore wigs on their heads, fashioned from human hair and topped with the feathers of parrots, cassowaries, eagles, kites and birds of paradise. The warriors thundered past in a cloud of dust and the clamour of rhythmic cries. They carried with them several sides of pork.

A few enquiries soon revealed what was happening. We had stumbled across a payback ceremony. One clan was paying compensation to another for killing one of their members during a tribal fight some months previously. Although much has changed in highland life since the first moments of contact in 1930, a great deal of original culture remains very much alive, and tribal warfare certainly comes within that category and nowhere more so than amongst the Huli people of the Southern Highlands.

Traditionally, Huli boys were raised and hardened up as warriors to defend and extend the interests of their family. Warfare was one of their main preoccupations in life. Today, as it was sixty years ago, it is still true to say that many clans live in a state of tension with their neighbours. Although open warfare is not as common now, it does periodically flare up. A drunken brawl, a pig wandering and damaging a neighbour's crops, a car accident on the developing network of rough dirt roads in the highlands, all have the potential to set off a major battle. Warfare was not and still is not seen by most people as a crime, merely as a way of setting things straight, of maintaining some kind of status quo.

Homemade shotguns have begun to change the nature and seriousness of this activity in some parts of the highlands, but much fighting is still conducted with bows and arrows and not very powerful ones at that. Injuries are common but on most occasions relatively few warriors die in battle. Once one or two people are killed a truce is often called and negotiations for peace started. As part of these negotiations compensation payments between the warring parties need to be worked out. If one side has killed opponents then the families of those opponents need to be paid or else they will more than likely take retaliatory action at a later date.

This is where the pigs come in. They form a large part of the compensation payment. They represent a clan's surplus productivity, in other words its wealth. Today, of course, there are other potential gifts including money. In the compensation ceremony we were shortly to witness about twenty pigs and the equivalent of a thousand pounds in cash were to be handed over as part payment of a large debt for the killing of one man. One of the problems of using pigs as currency is that a clan may not immediately have sufficient to meet its obligations, even though they can call in animals from relatives and others who may owe them favours. In the end this may turn out to be advantageous because it sometimes prolongs the payback period into months or even years. In this way the exchange of animals contributes to the stability of relations between clans, binding them together in ritual obligation. Occasionally, after full and final settlement has been reached, warfare has resumed almost immediately.

Of course the exchanges may backfire if not conducted properly, and that was one of the reasons so many armed warriors were on hand at the ceremony we witnessed. The presence of warriors in large numbers is also designed to overawe the enemy with a show of strength and firepower that will act as a deterrent against future attacks.

After butchering the pigs and deciding on exactly how much was to be given away and how much was to be kept back for a feast, unarmed clan members set off in procession for the exchange. The gifts were placed on a neutral piece of land while hundreds of people looked on. A couple of hundred metres apart the opposing groups of warriors stood and waited. Two nervous policemen watched over the total crowd of about 1000 people. Slowly an old man walked up and down the lines of pork proclaiming their value and offering them in payment. Suddenly there was a rush from the opposition warriors. One of the policemen leapt forward and dragged us back out of harm's way. The warriors swooped in on the pork and within seconds the ground was bare and the exchange over.

Throughout the highlands pigs play a central part in society and in some localities huge pig-giving festivals are held every few years. In this case there may be no compensation to pay. The pigs will have been raised to give away and impress neighbours, both friends and enemies. Human welfare and the fertility of crops and animals are all thought to depend on unseen influences such as magic, poison, personal betrayals and the proper or improper performance of rituals. To hold a great pig festival is to demonstrate that these are all under control, things are going well for the clan, and that its members are both numerous and prosperous. The preparations for such a show can take many years and when it happens may involve not only dancing and pig-giving but initiation and marriage ceremonies as well.

Individual men also use pigs for prestige and power. There are few traditional tribal chiefs in the highlands. Instead men who can accumulate, control and distribute wealth come to hold a certain amount of power and are called 'big men'. They use the pigs that their wives have raised as investment capital in the complicated network of social debts and credits that binds highland society together. The crucial point is that the wealth must be given away, and even more importantly, seen to be given away, for the individual to increase his influence in the region. In some areas live pigs get passed around in an almost continuous cycle of gift giving as each 'big man' and his group tries to outdo the others.

I witnessed one of these ceremonies outside Mount Hagen in 1989. Large numbers of people had gathered in a village square, including about 200 traditionally dressed warriors and women. Throughout the day these dancers bounced up and down chanting in unison. The scene was impressive. Each participant was soaked in glistening oil and from their necks hung sea-shells, brightly coloured necklaces, painted spirit boards, the fur of tree kangaroos and the tails of striped possums. Their faces were matt black, with fine lines of white or yellow, and a bright red nose often pierced and holding a large shell. On their heads they bore great wigs of woven cotton, cuscus fur, the feathers of eagles and kites and, most impressive of all, the long tail plumes of Princess Stephanie's and black sicklebill birds of paradise. The head-pieces were finished off with a final decoration of iridescent green beetles or pieces of Christmas tinsel that sparkled brightly in the tropical sun.

To the rhythmic beating of kundu drums this great mass of colour swayed up and down, up and down, all morning and for most of the afternoon too. The dancers seemed in a trance for much of the time, gazing unseeing into the air, their senses dulled by the chanting and the sheer exhaustion of keeping up the performance. Occasionally a relative would step forward and force a banana, a drink, or perhaps a cigarette into the mouth of one of the performers.

While the dance continued the 'big man' and his friends loudly proclaimed the exchange to take place. This oratory is almost as important as the gift-giving itself. Finally the pigs were paraded alive. They were tied to stakes down the centre of the village and an old man walked up and down and sang out the virtues of the animals before, amid a flurry of charging dancers, they were given away.

Across the highlands pigs occupy a central place wherever friend-ships are cemented, enemies assuaged, marriages celebrated, youths initiated and funerals held. The largest feasts, such as those held by the Chimbu people in Papua New Guinea and the Dani tribes in Irian Jaya, require the coordinated raising of hundreds of pigs over several years. This places quite a strain on other food-producing activities as the pigs are fed the bulk of the sweet potato crop. But such large feasts also have another detrimental effect on the health of the population. Pigs are not normally eaten in day-to-day life and the sudden consumption of large quantities of pork that may have been improperly cooked, or kept many days before finally being eaten, commonly leads to a disease called pigbel. This results from the multiplication in the intestine of *Clostridium* bacteria. Without antibiotics it can lead to a painful death.

In spite of their dependence on an imported vegetable as their staple crop and the central role of a non-native mammal in their culture, New Guinea highlanders still traditionally use much of the native fauna and flora in their lives. At ceremonies such as pig festivals their extraordinary costumes are like encyclopaedias of the surrounding natural history. These costumes vary from region to region but tend to have some common themes. Most obvious is the use of bird of paradise feathers in decoration. Some of these birds live surprisingly close to people. In the Tari valley blue, superb, and raggiana birds of paradise display in trees right in the midst of cultivated land and buildings. Single birds, or a display tree with several males, are often owned by one person, who will protect them until their plumes are sufficiently splendid for his needs. They will then be shot. In the past the traditional use of feathers does not seem to have damaged bird populations, but with the introduction of shotguns over the past few decades birds are now more easily killed. People are also wealthier so can afford to buy more plumes from hunters. However, there is very little hard and up to date evidence on which to assess the present impact on the populations of the birds.

Several tribes, including the Wola of the Southern Highlands, use king of Saxony bird of paradise plumes in their head-dresses. These are long thin wires with numerous tiny blue and white iridescent discs attached to them. The bird carries them on its head and waves them to and fro in courtship display. The Wola wave these feathers on their own heads in much the same way as the bird does and even imitate its call in their dancing.

In some parts of the island people have an even closer relationship with birds. The Dani believe that birds and men once lived in harmony together, neither recognising that the other was in any way different. Today each clan is affiliated with a particular species of bird who are considered to be clan members. Among Engan people certain birds are thought to be inhabited by ghosts. Their cries have specific meaning and if heard have to be obeyed. This may require some sort of ritual action or sacrifice to be performed. Failure to obey such an avian instruction is believed to cause sickness or death.

Some anthropologists have drawn parallels between birds of paradise and specific aspects of highland societies. For example, both people and birds use traditional dancing grounds to sing and display at certain times of year or in regular cycles. In the Wahgi valley it is only men that wear bird of paradise plumes just as in the birds themselves it is only the males that bear them. The men use these feathers in much the same way as the birds do, to attract female attention. A major function of their dancing displays, apart from the gift-giving, is a chance for the women to take a good look at the men from neighbouring clans and judge their appearance and performance and hence suitability for marriage. Among the Wahgi some people also believe that when men die they turn into birds.

The Huli of the Southern Highlands set their feathers in a most unusual wig. When boys become young men they begin to grow their hair out onto a frame. As the hair becomes longer it sits rather like a giant mushroom on their head and, after about eighteen months, they cut it and fashion it into a wig. The central decoration is usually the blue iridescent breast-plate of a superb bird of paradise, commonly surrounded by the tiny red and yellow feathers of a rainbow lorikeet. Older men also sport dozens of bright yellow or purple everlasting daisies. Crowning the wig is often a tuft of soft cassowary feathers out of which protrude the fine display plumes of several raggiana birds of paradise. Real extroverts have a whole pair of outstretched bird of prey wings perched in the top of their wig. The unusual thing about the Huli is that, unlike most other tribesmen, they still wear these head-dresses in their daily lives, even when shopping or doing business in the busy frontier town of Tari that lies in the heart of Huli territory. It can be quite a surprise bumping into one of these fellows in a supermarket or bank.

As human populations increase forests around the edges of the valleys are being steadily cleared to make way for new gardens. To obtain many of their feather decorations and other forest products the people need to make lengthy expeditions to the steep walls of their valleys and the mountains that rise above them. The natural history of the high altitude forests that grow there is the subject of the following chapter.

Chapter Ten

ISLANDS
in the AIR

*I*n the last hour of day a clinging drizzle creeps up from the valley below and drifts slowly over the hillside. It obscures the distant view and envelops the landscape in a soft veil. Tall beech trees stand as vague shadows, their topmost branches fading away into the mist. The evening air is cool and a steady breeze bites at exposed flesh. Nearby a waterfall thunders, heavy with the rain from an afternoon storm. Closer still, a sound resembling the rat-tat-tat of a machine-gun cuts through the air. This is a typical end to a day in the mountain forests of New Guinea.

This particular evening I was standing on the slopes just above the Tari Basin in the Southern Highlands, at an altitude of a little over 2000 metres. These mid-montane forests, as they are called to distinguish them from even higher vegetation, grow just above the level of possible cultivation. They cling to the valley walls and spill over the ridge-tops into gullies, ravines and sinkholes. They are a world apart from the warm green cathedrals of the lowland tropical rainforest. Here the climate is almost always overcast and gloomy. The trees appear twisted and dark in the mist, and great lumps of moss drip from every branch. And that machine-gun was the sound made by a rather unusual bird of paradise.

Many of the animals and plants that live in the mid-montane forests, or at any other altitude, are specifically adapted to the environment at that particular height. They cannot survive either in the warmer lands below or the cooler ones above. In this way each altitudinal zone is different from the next. Each is also cut off from similar habitats on other mountain ranges by the hostile climate of the intervening lowlands. They are, in effect, islands in the air.

The unique nature of the animal life in these mountain forests is soon apparent from the sounds alone. Some of the most conspicuous and unusual are the calls of the brown sicklebill, that bird of paradise with the machine-gun call. It's a large bird with a long, curved beak specially designed for probing under bark and into deep mats of moss in search of insect prey. It has even been seen to catch small frogs and lizards, and it also eats fruit. The female, as in most birds of paradise, is rather dull, mostly brown with a barred breast. The male has an iridescent blue-black back, a set of fine brown breast feathers that he can extend in display, and a long pointed tail, almost twice the length of his body. In the early morning and late afternoon he perches on high exposed branches, ruffles his display plumes and, in a motion that looks like a violent fit of coughing, utters his extraordinary call, presumably designed either to attract female attention or deter other male competitors.

The males are solitary and quite shy. With such a conspicuous tail they need to be because they are frequently hunted. Sicklebill tails are a favourite decoration in ceremonial head-dresses. The tail feathers of its close relative, the black sicklebill, are also sought by man. It's a similar bird, slightly larger, but with an even longer tail. It too is easily tracked down by its voice, to my mind one of the most beautiful of all the birds of paradise. It's composed of just two notes but they sound as though they have come from a powerful electric guitar rather than a bird. Unfortunately, because this species tends to live at a slightly lower altitude than the brown sicklebill, its habitat overlaps with the highest levels of cultivation. Not only is it threatened by hunting but also by extensive loss of habitat as more and more land is cleared for gardens.

The king of Saxony bird of paradise is another mid-montane species whose plumes are regularly used for personal adornment. Some are set in head-dresses but I have also seen them worn through a hole in the nose. People can do this easily because the plumes are very thin. Each is a wire about 40 centimetres long, with many tiny blue discs hanging from one side. The male bird carries these not on his tail but protruding from behind his ears. They are about twice the length of his body and hang down over his back while at rest. As he displays from a regular perch in a tall tree the male rotates these feathers back, forwards and sideways like a pair of mobile antennae. To increase the effectiveness of this he emits a call which has often been described as a combination of a faulty electrical appliance and static from a badly tuned radio.

None of these birds of paradise live anywhere else. They are confined to these islands of mountain forest. There are other animal groups which also have species adapted for a high altitude life. Several mammals, for example, specialise in living in the mountains and are not found lower down. There are two species of cuscus that are unique to the mountains – the silky cuscus and the mountain cuscus. These are even more cuddly in appearance than their lowland relatives as they have very thick pelts for keeping warm at these altitudes. The silky cuscus seems at first sight to be just a ball of shiny black fur. Its ears are almost completely hidden and its legs and face only just protrude beyond its dense coat. Like all cuscuses, it has a prehensile tail that is bare at the end. Using this, it can dangle upside down from a branch, with all four other limbs hanging completely free, and use its forepaws to feed on orchid leaves and other hanging vegetation.

The trees at these altitudes are often smothered in moss and the pygmy ringtail puts this to good use in home building. It's a small light brown possum confined to mountain forests, especially those with lots of moss. It uses it to build a delicate nest for its young, often in the fork of a tree. The smallest marsupial to live up here is another possum, the diminutive long-tailed pygmy possum. It weighs about 20 grammes, less than an ounce, and builds tiny nests woven out of leaves.

The largest is Doria's tree kangaroo which, like the cuscuses, tends to have rather thicker fur and a more rounded appearance than its relatives at lower altitudes. It inhabits forests a little lower down but is most common in the mountains of the central highlands where it lives right up to the tree line. It's the best climber of all the tree kangaroos and because of this has lost the ability to hop with both legs together. Weighing up to 18 kilogrammes it's a valuable catch for hunters. They pursue the animal by moonlight, using dogs to corner one before despatching it with an arrow or bullet. It's now rare in much of its range.

The strange animals and plants that live only at these altitudes add considerably to the total number of species on the island. But there's another way in which the mountains foster diversity. Animals living in forests at the same height but on different mountain ranges are effectively cut off from each other by the intervening lowlands. They are isolated as surely as if they were on islands surrounded by a sea of water. If a particular species has members on various mountains then each separate group will effectively be cut off from breeding with the others. They will eventually diverge in appearance and behaviour. Over thousands of years the isolated mountain populations become so different from each other that they are all classed as separate species. This has dramatically increased the overall variety of life on the island. Astrapia birds of paradise are characteristic inhabitants of the mid-montane forest and provide a good example of such speciation.

One of the most interesting species is called the ribbon-tailed astrapia. The males have tails that for their body size are the longest of any bird in the world. For a bird with a body of only 20 centimetres to carry a tail that may reach a metre in length is quite a feat. He does not seem to fly in a straight line but seems to undulate through the air, and then glide with the two feathers of his great white tail trailing out behind.

The ribbon-tailed astrapia was only discovered in 1939 and lives within a restricted range in the central highlands of Papua New Guinea. Other similar species of astrapia live on different mountain ranges. To the north-east lies the Huon Peninsula, separated from the central highlands by a broad valley that does not rise much above sea level. Trapped on that particular chunk of rock is the Huon astrapia, differing slightly in body colour from the ribbon-tail, and with a shorter purple-coloured tail. To the north-west in the Arfak Mountains lives the Arfak astrapia, very similar to the Huon bird in appearance but slightly different and placed in a separate species. To the west, in the Snow, Star, and Victor Emmanuel mountains, there's yet another, the splendid astrapia. And finally, the Princess Stephanie's astrapia, named in 1884 after the then crown princess of Austria, and confined to the eastern parts of the central ranges. Instead of a single original species of astrapia there are now five, each more or less isolated on different mountain ranges across the island.

Rather curiously, the Princess Stephanie's astrapia overlaps with the ribbon-tail in a few places. It seems unlikely that a common ancestor could have evolved into these two similar but separate species while they were living in the same place because they would have been forever interbreeding with each other. In fact hybrids between the two are not uncommon today. So perhaps they were once isolated on different mountain ranges and have only more recently expanded into the same areas. The overall effect of astrapia evolution has been a considerable increase in the diversity of birds of paradise on the island. This evolutionary process has been common in many animal and plant groups that live in these mountain forests.

In the mid-montane forests the vegetation is quite unlike that growing lower down. That's partly due to the cooler climate up here, but also because many of the plants have a different evolutionary history from those in the lowlands. The trees, shrubs and other plants of the lowland rainforests have their closest living relatives in the forests of South East Asia. But in the mid-montane forests the great southern beech trees that dominate many of these mountains have their nearest relatives in New Zealand and South America. Today these sites are many thousands of kilometres apart but at one time they were all close together, on the great southern supercontinent of Gondwanaland. As the various pieces of land that made up that supercontinent drifted apart they carried with them similar groups of plants that today survive wherever the fragments of Gondwanaland have ended up.

In fact these forests contain a mixture of plants derived from various continents with the Gondwanan elements introducing a very distinctive character to the vegetation. Among the southern beeches grow ancient-looking tree ferns and dense stands of bamboo. The fallen logs on the forest floor are covered in mats of bright green moss, brilliant white, red or yellow finger-like fungi, and ferns of a variety of size and shape rarely seen elsewhere. On the trees themselves hang great gardens of epiphytes, orange and red moss, pale lichen, the drooping fronds of bird's nest and maidenhair ferns so familiar in Europe as houseplants, and the delicate leaves of filmy ferns only one cell thick. One large beech tree can support 300 to 400 species of epiphytic plant. Unlike parasites, epiphytes do not feed off their hosts, but simply live on them.

Most varied and beautifully dainty of all are the orchids. New Guinea boasts over 2500 species, the greatest diversity of which is found in these montane forests. Few grow directly from the ground. Most are epiphytes, using other plants for support but doing them no harm in the process. It's an ideal habitat, away from the gloomy forest floor and in a good position to take in sunlight and the other necessities of life. The frequent rains wash nutrients down the trunks of the trees on which the orchids grow. By intercepting these the flowers have no need of soil.

They range in colour from white, through shades of yellow and blue, to pinks and reds. Most are tiny and many are shaped in bizarre ways, with long petals sticking out at strange angles and twisted in odd orientations. Presumably most of this architecture is designed to attract specific pollinating insects, but the biology of the vegetation is so poorly known that few of the pollinators have ever been observed.

Here the forest also contains many plants that are either directly useful to the people living in the valleys below, or have given rise to plants that are now domesticated and grown in their gardens. The number of wild gingers, for example, is extremely large. They vary from small, forest floor types to giant shrubs, and include climbing and epiphytic species as well. Their various fruits, often orange or red, provide splashes of colour in many an otherwise gloomy corner of the forest. *Pandanus* palms, otherwise known as screwpines, are typical at this altitude. During the nutting season large numbers of people trek many kilometres from their homes to particular trees they lay claim to. The round journey may take a number of days and with each nut cluster weighing several kilogrammes only a few can be carried back at a time. As a result they are quite expensive in the local markets and are usually sold only in small portions.

As altitude increases the trees become shorter and the moss on the lower branches and on the ground becomes thicker. At some point, often debated by botanists but around 3000 metres, mid-montane forest turns into upper montane or, as it's more commonly called, moss forest. Everything is festooned in a rich carpet of damp and shiny moss. This even seems to be a substitute for soil. The roots of trees grow not directly into the ground but first through great mounds of moss a metre or two thick.

Some animals are entirely at home up here, especially birds. Male Archbold's bower birds use the tangled architecture of the forest to help build a dancing arena. They pick a spot where the ground is reasonably clear but overhung by low branches. Below these they build a mat of dark coloured ferns and place on it a few snail shells, berries and bits of fungus. Occasionally they manage to collect the display plume of a King of Saxony bird of paradise and add this to the mat. They then drape the overhanging branches with the long but rather dull stems of certain types of forest orchid. The whole effect is so shabby and blends in so well with the surroundings that, although the structure may be a metre or more tall and double that in width, it's entirely possible to walk right past without noticing. The female presumably finds it irresistible.

Snakes do not find travel through this sort of habitat a problem, but being cold-blooded creatures a cool mountain climate isn't ideal for them. The rare Boelen's python, however, only found in the mountains of New Guinea, survives up at these heights, as well as in forests a little lower down. It's probably the only python in the world able to live at such high altitudes. The scales on its back are velvety black and the dark colour may help the snake absorb precious solar radiation. In sunlight they glow and shimmer with all the colours of the rainbow.

Another curious group of animals that live in these mountain forests are weevils of the genus *Gymnopholus*. Weevils are small beetles with long snorkel-like snouts and they are found in large numbers all over the world. But these particular ones are rather exceptional because they support a whole ecosystem on their backs. Fungi, algae, lichens, liverworts and mosses all grow on the exoskeletons of these peculiar insects. But even more remarkable than this are the animals that live here too. Rotifers, nematode worms, protozoa, mites and springtails all inhabit the miniaturised vegetation that thrives on the weevils' bodies. This bizarre combination of life is, as far as anyone knows, unique to the high altitude weevils of New Guinea.

The higher the altitude the cooler the climate, and up beyond the moss forest the mountains support yet another zone of life with a whole new range of animals and plants. The vegetation becomes much more open, with patches of stunted woodland interspersed with sub-alpine grasslands and herbfields. No longer are southern beech and *Pandanus* common. Instead trees like southern pine, celery topped pine and native cedar dominate. They stand in clumps sheltering low bushes beneath them. On the ground grow tussock grasses, beds of miniature ferns and a whole variety of tiny flowers.

With a clear alpine atmosphere and no canopy overhead a sunny day at this altitude reveals a scene of almost magical quality, as I discovered one morning, on a ridge at about 3500 metres in the Star Mountains. It was around eight o'clock and the clouds and rain that inevitably build up during the day had yet to arrive. The distant peaks of Mount Capella were shining brightly in the low sunlight, but it was the vegetation that captured my attention. The colours were extraordinary. No longer, as in the dim forests below, was green the dominant hue. The clustered needles of the southern pines were clad in a sheen of white in the early morning sun. From their branches hung great clumps of moss, some orange, others red, brown or purple. Their trunks were plastered with greyish lichen and from their bark grew bright red epiphytic flowers shaped like miniature trumpets. Below them stood bushes with thick waxy leaves, their shiny surfaces a protection against the high altitude light intensity. At the top of each bush the leaves were a deep red while at the bottom they were green. Many were in flower and sported delicate pink blossoms. Patches of bare earth beneath the trees were covered in mats of brilliant white lichen while in other places, hidden among the tough grasses, grew tiny sub-alpine flowers with petals of blue, red, yellow or white.

All these plants grow only within a limited altitudinal range. That's also true of many of the birds of the sub-alpine woodlands. This is a much easier place for bird watching than lower down the mountains because the habitat is so open. Flowering bushes are particularly good spots to wait and watch. They are visited by honeyeaters and lorikeets wanting to feast on the sweet nectar. There's considerable competition for a good clump of flowers and they are worth fighting for. I have watched a single black-throated honeyeater vigorously defending a flowering umbrella tree again and again against the attentions of flocks of hungry plum-faced lorikeets.

The hanging moss also provides a rich feeding ground for birds because it shelters all kinds of little insects. Small parties of black sitellas, rather like treecreepers, scurry over, under and along moss-laden branches probing for a meal.

But perhaps the most unusual bird confined to these heights is the Macgregor's bird of paradise. It feeds largely on the fruits of southern pines which is one of the reasons it cannot live at lower altitudes. It's confined to the Snow, Star, and Owen Stanley mountains at heights of between about 2900 and 4000 metres and is one of the most atypical of all the birds of paradise. The male does not have any gaudy display plumes; nor does he have a loud or elaborate voice. In fact both male and female are virtually identical, both black with large yellow wattles around the eyes and with yellow patches on their wings. Unlike the more typical birds of paradise males of this species are monogamous and spend most of their time with their partner. They forage in close company, roost together, and if separated greet each other on their reunion with a brief, wing fluttering ritual and gentle calls.

Their specialised diet may be related to their unusual social behaviour. If southern pine fruits are not sufficiently abundant and nutritious for the female alone to raise her young then the male may have to help her. If this were the case he could not be promiscuous in the way many other male birds of paradise are. The only reported study of Macgregor's bird of paradise at a nest does indeed report that the male helped his mate in feeding the chicks.

The progression of different habitats as altitude increases is not a straightforward one. For example, above the sub-alpine woodlands grassland tends to predominate, but there are also large areas of grass at lower elevations too. Flying over any highland regions above 3000 metres, patches of grassland entirely enclosed by mountain forests are a common sight. Most tend to be in shallow valleys. Frosts collect here and could be a factor encouraging their presence.

But there's another possible explanation: fire. Although they tend to be very wet, people do manage to set light to the grass, sometimes while hunting, sometimes, it seems, just for fun, and natural fires also occur.

Many of these sub-alpine valleys contain extensive 'savannas' of tree ferns. Some grow as high as real trees but most stand about only 2 metres tall. They give these isolated grasslands a primeval feel, for these are plants with an ancient history. When the dinosaurs first appeared on earth there were no flowering plants and no typical trees. Instead plants very similar to these tree ferns were common in the landscape. Although they survive in the understorey of many tropical forests, New Guinea is now the only place with extensive savannas in which they predominate. They tend to grow on well-drained slopes, often on the sides of gullies carved out by small streams.

A curious feature of these places is that they receive a great amount of rain but often seem to have no obvious exit through which a river could flow. In the Star Mountains I have seen a large stream spring from a cave halfway up the slopes of a grassy valley, tumble down a waterfall, and then simply end in a small lake with no outflow. Where does all the water go? Presumably, either into sink-holes or simply down through the porous rocks. Many of these areas have a very bumpy appearance because they are covered with hillocks and depressions. Each of the depressions probably contains a small soak-away or sink-hole of its own.

The grasslands above the sub-alpine woodland merge into bogs and fens dotted with small tarns. Tussock grass, dwarf ferns and low mounds of moss cover most of the ground. Here and there tiny alpine flowers bloom. Many of the flowers that grow at this height are relatives of species found in the Himalayas, New Zealand, or even the Alps of Europe. These mountain ranges are separated by many thousands of kilometres with no alpine habitats in between. But during past ice ages alpine vegetation was able to spread to much lower altitudes and some of the smaller summits in between major mountain ranges would also have experienced alpine conditions. Seeds could have travelled from one peak to the next on the feathers or in the guts of birds. Over many thousands of years plants from distant mountain ranges could have become established far from their origins.

On other tropical mountains, such as those in East Africa, many species are found only on individual peaks. But in New Guinea most of the alpine species are spread across most of the mountain ranges, and about a third of them are also found outside New Guinea. This suggests that the plants have not had time since their arrival to speciate on their respective mountain tops which also implies that they have arrived relatively recently, probably only during the last ice-age.

One of the most extensive areas of alpine grassland on the island is on Mount Giluwe, an extinct lava-shield volcano that rises to 4368 metres in Papua New Guinea. Its craggy summit is the weathered remains of a large plug of lava poking up in the air. As molten lava flowed out and down the slope of the volcano many hundreds of thousands of years ago it created a series of gently sloping plateaux which have since been ground down by glaciers. Now that the glaciers have retreated huge shallow bowls remain. These contain grasslands dotted with dozens of peaty tarns. The scenery is similar to what you would expect to see in the highlands of Scotland or the mountains of New Zealand rather than on a tropical island.

The whole feel of the place is cold, bleak and very wet. The dawn may be clear but within a few hours cloud almost inevitably bubbles up from the damp rainforests below. It climbs over ridge after ridge until the entire mountain is covered in a damp, clinging blanket of cloud. When the rain comes, as it does almost every afternoon, it is with the fury of a tropical downpour but the temperature of a temperate hailstorm. The water rushes down the mountainside in sheets, in places disappearing underground, carving out deep tunnels through the peat. The water on level patches of ground, never more than a centimetre or two beneath the surface, now stands as a visible sheet on top of it.

When the rain stops life suddenly resumes. Frogs croak around the pools, alpine pipits take to the air and tiny moths flutter in the grass. Even some mammals live at these heights. The waterlogged ground shows signs of burrowing by rodents. How they manage to avoid drowning in these holes is something of a mystery. They are hunted by New Guinea wild dogs, similar to the Australian dingo and introduced thousands of years ago by mankind. The dogs are shy and very rarely seen by people but their wailing calls are often heard at night drifting over the highest valleys and slopes. During the day I have watched spotted marsh harriers coursing the grass lands, presumably also for rodent prey. A few marsupials survive up here too. Close to the edge of alpine woodlands mountain walla-bies come out to graze. Copper ringtail possums and long-beaked echidnas have also been seen out on high boggy grasslands.

Dwarf rhododendrons are common. One species stands no more than shoe high, growing as a low round cushion from which sprout tiny red trumpet-shaped flowers. Bright blue gentians nestle low among the tussock grass. Small daisy-like flowers sprout around the edge of tarns, and clusters of tiny blooms rather like miniature buttercups seem to sit directly on the damp ground. The problems such plants face on a high tropical mountain are somewhat different from those in the Alps or Himalayas. They are not buried beneath snow or ice for part of the year, but instead must face tempera-tures that may range from as high as 20°C down to freezing in a single day.

It comes as quite a surprise to find glacial landscapes only a few hundred kilometres from the equator but on Mount Giluwe they are in evidence everywhere. At one time the mountain supported over 180 square kilometres of glacier. The entire summit area above 3200 metres was covered by an ice cap during the last glaciation and smaller glaciers tumbled down into valleys below. Their scars remain, the pattern of scouring clearly visible on the modern land-scape. Most impressive of all are the deep U-shaped valleys descend-ing from the summit. They end in great piles of rock called terminal moraines. They are now forested hillocks but once they were debris carried down the mountainside on the snouts of the glaciers.

On Mount Jaya, the highest peak of the island, glaciers still cover the rocks. It is part of Irian Jaya's main range, appropriately called the Snow Mountains. The actual summit is a craggy grey spike of limestone named Carstenz Pyramid after the explorer, Jan Carstenz, who first reported seeing snow on the mountains of New Guinea in 1623. Just below it stretch several snowfields and extensive sheets of ice. The glaciers spill off the mountain top, clinging to steep rock-faces or descending into barren glacial valleys. In places the brilliant white of the ice is dotted with a series of remarkable, bright blue pools of meltwater. The whole scene is one that seems startlingly out of place on a tropical island. Glaciers, hardly a stone's throw from steamy lowland rainforests, and within sight of a warm coral sea. It is a dramatic geographical contrast, unique in the world.

The rocks from which this high mountain is made were laid down on an ocean floor about twenty million years ago. They have been pushed up to their present height only in the last few million years. In other words, they are geologically very young mountains. At 4884 metres Mount Jaya is higher than any other peak in South East Asia, Australasia or the Pacific. On three sides it is surrounded by towering 1000-metre cliffs of contorted, dark grey rock. To the south and east these plunge directly into thick tropical jungle, while to the north their base meets a plateau of mountain forests and grassland that rolls away to the horizon. The fourth side slopes down gradually to the height of the rest of the range but is dramatically dissected by a pair of deep, steep-sided valleys carved by glaciers sometime in the past.

While flying low over the summit area in a helicopter I estimated that the snow and ice now cover a total area of about 4 or 5 square kilometres. The last accurate calculation was by an Australian expedition in 1972. At that time the figure was just under 7 square kilometres. For at least the last hundred years the glaciers have been shrinking because of a general increase in world temperatures. That retreat is now rapid and will probably result in the disappearance of permanent ice from the mountain within the next few decades. During this century there have been three other glacier-clad summits in Irian Jaya: Mount Trikora, Mount Indenburg and Mount Mandala. Mount Trikora lost its ice sometime around 1960, and Mounts Mandala and Indenburg only a year or two ago. All of them still receive occasional snow but that usually melts within a few hours or days.

At the height of the last ice age there would have been about 1000 square kilometres of glaciers on the Snow Mountains. The evidence of that previous ice cover is dramatically visible all around: steep-sided, ice-gouged valleys; splintered crags shattered by frost; deep, ice-carved bowls called cirques, and large piles of rocky debris called moraines, some of which are over 200 metres high.

Where the present-day glaciers are retreating they are exposing fresh rock which provides new opportunities for plants. At this height bare rock becomes colonised by tundra vegetation: mosses, lichens and a few tuft grasses and sedges. On the ice itself grow colonies of algae. This mountain, only 450 kilometres from the equator, supports plants that we more commonly think of as belonging to the Arctic. It's the mountain building that has made this particular island truly special, that sets it apart from all the other tropical islands in Australasia, South East Asia and the Pacific.

But the mountain building has brought other consequences too. Not far from the summit of Mount Jaya lies a massive body of copper and gold ore. The great forces that pushed these summits up have also made them rich in minerals. Remote as it is, that ore is now the centre of a huge industrial operation, the Freeport mine. It seems that even the most isolated spots on the island are now feeling the influence of the twentieth century.

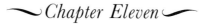

Chapter Eleven

THE END

OF

ISOLATION

*T*he deafening blast of a siren shatters the mountain air. A massive machine, the size of an apartment block, creaks forward on caterpillar tracks through thigh-deep mud. It repositions itself against a wall of rock and extends an arm. A giant shovel at the end of the arm claws at the rockface, scooping up 30 tonnes in a single sweep and dumping it in a waiting truck. The truck itself is enormous, with tyres taller than a man, and capable of carrying over 175 tonnes of rock and earth at a time. A row of these vehicles queue up at the shovel. Every 2 minutes or so another 175 tonnes of mountainside is carted away.

This is Ok Tedi copper and gold mine in the remote Star Mountains of Papua New Guinea. Twenty years ago this area had barely been explored. The first government patrol had entered the region in only 1963. The few people that lived among these precipitous slopes knew virtually nothing of the outside world. They hunted, grew crops in forest clearings, and performed rituals in spirit houses just as their ancestors had done for untold numbers of generations. The men wore just a single article of clothing – a gourd stuck over their penis and tied round their waist with twine.

Then in 1968 prospectors entered the mountains using helicopters to land in otherwise inaccessible spots. They found traces of copper in the Ok Tedi river. Ok Tedi has now become the fifth largest copper mine in the world. Today, daily flights link the Star Mountains with the rest of the world and satellites flash communications from here to the stock exchanges of Sydney, New York and other centres of global finance. Within two decades these remote mountainsides, their people and wildlife have been shot from obscurity to a prominent place in the cash economy of the late twentieth century. Such is the fate and the future of many parts of this tropical island.

Development has been a long time coming to New Guinea but it is now underway at breakneck speed. Before the Second World War most of the island had been left alone by its colonial masters, the Dutch in the west and the Australians in the east. The malarious climate, an extraordinarily rugged topography and local inhabitants who were often hostile conspired to keep most white men confined to the margins of New Guinea. There were extensive copra and coconut plantations on the coast and a few individuals had been lured into the interior by the promise of gold. Missionaries were very active but were constrained by the same factors that held everybody else back. It was truly a place that time had, if not entirely forgotten, certainly left alone.

Since the Second World War all that has changed, partly through political and economic will, but also through the use of new technology. Anti-malarial drugs have made low-lying areas safer places to live, and light aircraft and helicopters have enabled even the most rugged and remote parts of the highlands to be explored and developed. In some cases the pioneers have been missionaries; in others government patrols and expeditions. But most dramatic in their achievements have undoubtedly been the miners. Since Mick Leahy discovered the hidden highland valleys in the 1930s the search for gold and copper has opened up some of the most spectacular and difficult locations in the world.

It has not been easy or cheap to extract riches from New Guinea. Ok Tedi, for example, is not only remote, it suffers from earthquakes and landslips and phenomenal rainfall – over 10 metres a year. Under these conditions the costs have been horrendous. It took over one and a half billion US dollars to get this particular project up and running. Geological and environmental problems still lurk around almost every corner. But the potential rewards of mining in New

Guinea are enormous and that's what has driven the exploration.

The rocks are rich in minerals because of the violent geological activity out of which the island was born. As Pacific Ocean crust slid beneath the advancing landmass of Australia it began to heat and melt and in the process certain minerals became concentrated. The same forces buckled and twisted the great mountain ranges of the island, creating fractures and faults in the overlying rocks. The mineralised ores were extruded through these channels towards the surface. In New Guinea this has happened in hundreds of places, and in several the minerals are sufficiently concentrated to be worth the effort of mining.

By the nature of their formation they tend to be in some of the most rugged and remote country. There is even a huge mine just beneath the glacier-clad peaks of Mount Jaya, the highest mountain on the island. It contains not only copper but also gold and silver in impressive quantities. In June 1991 the Freeport company that runs the site announced fresh estimates for the amount of gold they hope to extract. These new figures reveal that the rocks which they're mining contain quite simply the largest known reserves of gold in the world.

It's perhaps ironic that the very processes which built this island into such a rugged and inaccessible place are now contributing so significantly to the opening of its most wild frontiers. That opening up is not without its problems. There's already been a good deal of controversy over the dumping of waste into the local river system at Ok Tedi. This eventually ends up in the River Fly. The government and the company have reached a compromise solution, balancing pollution against mine productivity and profitability. Wastes from the mine are allowed into the river system but at certain predetermined levels which are not supposed to be breached. The environmental damage is weighed against the economic benefits that the mine brings. These are considerable: in 1989 over 40 per cent of Papua New Guinea's total export earnings came from this single mine. Around Ok Tedi the local people have also received material benefits and a chance to hop on the train of economic development.

With more and more massive development planned in many of the island's wildest locations what is the future for the wildlife, environment and people of New Guinea? At the moment this is still one of the world's last true wilderness areas. Estimates of the amount of land that remains forested vary but somewhere between 70 and 80 per cent is a reasonable guess, a remarkably high proportion. In fact, it is the most extensive area of tropical rainforest still standing in South East Asia. Because of its large range of habitats the island is also one of the world's 'biodiversity hotspots'. In other words it contains one of the most varied collections of animals and plants on earth. New species are being discovered every year. So far, most do not face imminent extinction, unlike the inhabitants of many tropical forests elsewhere.

The future is difficult to predict because the picture is changing so fast. It's further complicated because conditions are quite different on either side of the international border that splits the island in two. So far, mining has levelled a few mountains, destroyed some relatively small areas of forest and polluted several river systems, but the other major extractive activity on the island has the potential to have a much wider impact.

Logging is finally beginning to hit New Guinea in a big way. Because it is remote and undeveloped the island has so far been spared the extensive destruction suffered by other areas of tropical forest. Extraction costs are high and its forests are not as rich in commercial species of tree as those of the rest of Asia. With most other forests in the region set to be logged out within a few decades, however, the attention of logging companies is turning to New Guinea.

At the moment Irian Jaya is less developed than Papua New Guinea. It's over 80 per cent forested. But in 1990 development budgets were tripled and much of this money is targeted at the exploitation of Irian Jaya's massive natural wealth. Already the Vogelkop Peninsula is suffering from considerable logging activity and one of the largest remaining areas of mangrove forests in the world, Bintuni Bay, is being steadily felled. Elsewhere there are plans to replace thousands of hectares of natural forest with eucalyptus plantations. The Planning and Development Board has said it is willing to overlook environmental matters in order to 'reduce harassment' to developers. Moreover, the Indonesian government has often ignored the wishes of local Irianese people, even shifting them wholesale from areas it proposes to exploit. The future of many of Irian Jaya's lowland forests and the people that live within them could be bleak in the decades ahead.

In Papua New Guinea the situation is far more confused. Government policy is muddled and many of the decisions affecting the future of the forests have taken place directly between foreign logging companies and local landowners. This means that local people can have a say and a share in any reward, but it has also enabled foreign and national businesses to deceive and cheat local landowners who rarely understand what they are letting themselves in for. To add to the confusion some of the government ministers and officials who have been involved in the industry have been assisting timber companies in return for illegal bribes. As some of these companies have budgets many times the size of the entire annual expenditure of the government of Papua New Guinea their power is potentially overwhelming.

A recent investigation by a well-respected judge began to uncover many of the details behind these shady dealings. As the horror stories of corruption at the highest levels of government began to emerge, and prosecution proceedings started to look likely, the office containing the written evidence conveniently caught fire. No further action has been taken and the final report has not been published in Papua New Guinea. Briefly, in 1989, there was renewed hope when the government declared a ban on new timber cutting as part of the worldwide Tropical Forests Action Plan. Then soon after that was announced several new timber licences were issued.

The future is unclear, but if the recent past is any indication it's not too rosy for the lowland rainforests of Papua New Guinea. Over the past decade the export of timber has increased over six-fold. In the process there has been considerable social disruption and massive environmental degradation in the areas concerned. Perhaps one of the worst aspects of all is that neither local people nor national government receive a decent financial return. Much of the timber is exported as raw logs, 90 per cent to Japan, Taiwan and South Korea. Because they have not been processed in any way they have a relatively low value, which in many cases has been further decreased by the questionable accounting practices of several of the giant corporations involved. Laws were introduced in 1989 to ban the export of certain valuable tree species as raw logs. But, on the other hand, the budget and staff of the Department of Forests have been steadily cut over the past decade so enforcement of this and other legislation is patchy and ineffective. If the future continues as in the recent past, Papua New Guinea stands to lose a sizeable proportion of its lowland forests in a largely uncontrolled manner.

In the struggle to protect the natural environment this island enjoys one great advantage over many other tropical areas. At the moment most wild habitat still remains intact. The opportunity to save vast tracts of wilderness is still an option here. But what active steps are being taken, both in Irian Jaya and Papua New Guinea, to protect this natural heritage? Perhaps one of the most hopeful aspects of the New Guinea situation is the sheer remoteness and rugged nature of much of the island. It's hard to imagine some chunks of landscape being of any use at all, except perhaps for traditional hunting. Many of the forests are not only rugged but also of very low grade timber. Even if world timber prices soar, as they must surely do, it's not likely that it will ever be economically feasible to log all the forests. This is especially true in the mountains.

Traditionally the Melanesian people have had a close affinity with their land and that's another potential plus on the side of conservation. In Papua New Guinea over 95 per cent of the land is traditionally owned and, with over 80 per cent of the population still following an agricultural life, most people are strongly tied to the local ecology of their land. People not only own their homes and immediate gardens but also have complicated rights passed on through the generations to use wild forest for hunting and collecting. They may also regard remote mountainsides as sacred or special places.

This does, however, cause one significant problem. The government finds it hard to create national parks because people will not sell their land and generally demand exorbitant rents for its use. Only 2 per cent of Papua New Guinea is protected in any sort of park. On the other hand, traditional ownership means the government cannot steamroller development through against local opposition. In some cases village land tenure can be turned to very positive advantage in the protection of wild places.

The Papua New Guinea government was one of the first to recognise the potential value of local participation in wildlife conservation. It has put this into practice through a series of Wildlife Management Areas. The traditional landowners are allowed to use the areas as they have always done but are encouraged to create certain rules covering its use. These are aimed at keeping outsiders away and preventing the owners themselves from over-exploiting their natural resources. The idea is to encourage people to utilise wildlife in a sustainable way.

One classic example is a megapode nesting ground on the island of New Britain. It's called Pokili (see Chapter 1). The eggs from the Pokili nesting ground have been harvested for as long as anyone can remember. People dig out the megapode tunnels and retrieve the eggs from the volcanically heated soil. Traditionally the eggs were eaten by the collectors and their families. Now there's a cash economy on the island and so they are also sold at market. This has led to over-harvesting. During the 1970s it was estimated that about six million eggs were being collected every year. Yields declined as fewer and fewer chicks managed to hatch and grow to adulthood. In the past there had been certain taboos restricting the type of person allowed to collect eggs, but these were not sufficiently strong to prevent the situation deteriorating. This was why the villagers were keen to introduce controls.

In 1975 the government and local people created the Pokili Wildlife Management Area. Hunting the birds themselves is now forbidden; only landowners can take eggs, and harvesting is prohibited in August to allow sufficient young birds to hatch and maintain the population. Since 1975 a further rule has been introduced, restricting egg collecting to just Tuesdays, Thursdays and Saturdays. The rules are set and enforced by a committee of local elders.

The idea is an excellent one as it allows the owners of the land to obtain an income from the land while preserving the wildlife as an ever renewing resource. It also allows for the development of other income sources such as tourism. Enforcement is not strict, however, so many of the rules are broken, and local people still complain of dwindling harvests. Although villagers are keen to see the system work, they no longer receive support from the government in their efforts to preserve the area. The Department of Environment and Conservation is now one of the most poorly funded of all ministries. Without that back-up the situation looks likely to deteriorate.

Elsewhere there has been a slightly different approach to Wildlife Management Areas. The Tonda area includes the plains of the Bensbach region (see Chapter 6). It was selected as the site of a potential wildlife reserve in the 1960s because of its rich bird life. But local people were not keen to sell their land. Instead a series of rules and incentives were established to encourage the landowners to keep the area wild. Any person with traditional rights to the area is permitted to hunt or fish. The area is huge, rich in game, and the human population is low so this poses no problem. As additional incentives, which add more value to the wildlife, royalties are paid by visiting tourists and hunters. Although small in total amount, these payments are just about the only way for people to make any cash in this remote corner of the country. So far, the area remains as wild as ever, a true wilderness.

Cash has also been used as a tool to protect specific animals outside formal management areas. Crocodile eggs are harvested in the Sepik region, and the income they generate encourages the preservation of both the crocodiles and their habitat (see Chapter 8). A similarly novel approach has also helped butterfly conservation. The forests of New Guinea contain some of the most spectacular butterflies in the world including the largest, the Queen Alexandra's birdwing. Colourful butterflies are much in demand by collectors and butterfly houses around the world. Here in Papua New Guinea they have worked out a way of supplying that demand without depleting butterfly populations. At the same time the scheme provides an incentive to preserve local forests.

In areas of old abandoned gardens, forest clearings or open river banks butterflies congregate in large numbers. To induce them to stay and lay eggs villagers plant these areas with certain flowers and other plants. These provide nectar for the adults and food for their caterpillars. Such a 'butterfly farm', well stocked with a variety of plants, has the potential to sustain a butterfly population that can be harvested at regular intervals without ill effect. The local forest is important because it supplies new immigrants. Often the butterflies are collected from the 'farm' as pupae and then hatched in captivity. This ensures perfect specimens. Wild animals have effectively been turned into a cash crop and in the process both the butterfly population and the surrounding forest have become valuable commodities to be looked after and protected with care.

But, in spite of these community participation projects in Papua New Guinea, the conservation of natural resources receives very little attention and money from the government. At the moment, habitats and wildlife are often protected more by accident than by design.

In Irian Jaya conservation takes place against a very different political background. Indonesia took over control of the province from the Dutch in 1963. There followed a period of considerable repression against the native population who are culturally different from Indonesians. As well as mining and logging the Indonesian government has been promoting the transmigration of huge numbers of its citizens from more crowded islands such as Java to its outlying provinces, including Irian Jaya. This has done little if anything to relieve overcrowding and environmental degradation on the islands from which the migrants come, but has often caused problems at their destination. In Irian Jaya it has also contributed to watering down the cultural identity of this remote and often rebellious province. The indigenous people are being further swamped by a tide of thousands of unofficial immigrants from the rest of Indonesia. These new arrivals take most of the available jobs and opportunities.

Until recently there was little economic activity in the province but that is changing fast. Irian Jaya is about to enter the twentieth century in a big way. The government has now divided the land into areas designated for various development activities: mining; logging; transmigration settlements; national parks, etc. On the benefit side this means that, working from a map, almost all the area of which is still forested, the authorities have been able to designate about 20 per cent of the total as protected areas. By any country's standards that is a very significant proportion of land.

Some of the reserves are of global importance. The Arfak Mountains in the north-west have dazzled naturalists from the midnineteenth century onwards with their variety of unusual plant and animal life. They contain several unique birds of paradise as well as the greatest concentration of birdwing butterfly species on the island. Part of the mountains are now protected in the Arfak Nature Reserve.

The proposed Lorentz National Park is of international importance because of its size and variety of habitats. Stretching from the peak of the highest mountain on the island down to the coast below, it encloses a massive 14 832 square kilometres of land. Within its boundaries 34 different types of ecosystem have been identified, from glaciers to tidal mangrove swamps. It is probably the only protected area in the tropics with such a huge variety of landscapes and habitats.

Unfortunately some of the proposed protected areas are already being violated by roads, mines, oil exploration and other projects before they have been created. This does not augur well for their long-term future. New parks are regularly being created or upgraded, however, and in several the indigenous people are being encouraged to be involved in such a way that they can benefit from nature conservation. There has been some success in the Arfak Nature Reserve where most of the forest protection is now carried out by the local inhabitants. These villagers also engage in butterfly farming around the reserve to produce a cash income from the forest. In the Cyclops Mountains Nature Reserve near Jayapura, the Cenderawasih Bay Marine Nature Reserve, and the new Wasur National Park, local community participation projects are also under way. Active conservation is certainly pushing ahead here and the World Wide Fund for Nature is very actively involved in the province. But there is still a lot to be achieved before the protected area network in Irian Jaya is complete and secure. Whether the parks will become a real success, protecting wildlife against the onslaught of massive mechanised development projects, while at the same time providing opportunity for local inhabitants, is still a matter open to debate.

The island of New Guinea has been continuously settled by humans for 40 000 years. For at least the last 10 000, people have been clearing forests and altering the landscape to grow crops. Much of the forest on the island shows some evidence of past disturbance. In spite of that history most of the island has remained wild and unassailable well into this century. Only in the highland valleys had major tracts of land been stripped of their native vegetation before white men arrived.

The people here have always had a close affinity with the land, its vegetation and wildlife. It provided them with fertile soils for their gardens, materials to construct their homes, and wild animals and plants to be used not only as food and clothing but in ritual and display as well. In spite of all this the forests were preserved not so much out of foresight or choice but because a small population working with stone tools alone was incapable of clearing more.

Populations are now growing rapidly. Papua New Guinea has one of the fastest human growth rates in the world, about 2.5 per cent a year. Pressure for agricultural land, especially in the highlands, is now intense. Cash crops such as coffee, tea and even cattle are demanding of land in several parts of the country. In Irian Jaya population densities are lower but are being increased by immigration. At the same time as populations are expanding rapidly other dramatic changes are sweeping across the island at an even faster rate. New Guinea has a wealth of untapped natural resources: gold; silver; copper; oil; natural gas and timber. At the moment there's a scramble for these riches, both in Papua New Guinea and Irian Jaya. In only the past four decades the landscapes of the island have seen more changes than in the forty millennia of previous human impact. Some of the people of the island are benefiting from these changes, many more are not.

New Guinea has one of the greatest concentrations of exciting natural history and rich human culture in the world. Both face turbulent change. Several observers have made the comment that New Guinea is at a crossroads in its history. It seems to me that it is already on the motorway, careering away from its past towards a distant and uncertain future.

BIBLIOGRAPHY

Beehler Bruce M, Pratt Thane K, Zimmerman Dale A. *Birds of New Guinea*. Princeton University Press, 1986.

Blong RJ. *The Time of Darkness*. Australian National University Press, 1982.

Brown Paula. *Highland Peoples of New Guinea*. Cambridge University Press, 1978.

Coates Brian J. *The Birds of Papua New Guinea* (volumes I and II). Dove Publications, 1985 and 1990.

Collingridge George. *The First Discovery of Australia and New Guinea*. Pan Books, 1982.

Collins N Mark, Sayer Jeffrey A, Whitmore Timothy C (eds). *The Conservation Atlas of Tropical Forests; Asia and the Pacific*. Macmillan Press Ltd, 1991.

Connolly Bob, Anderson Robin. *First Contact*. Viking, 1987.

Cooper WT, Forshaw J. *The Birds of Paradise and Bowerbirds*. Collins, 1977.

Denoon Donald, Snowden Catherine. *A Time to Plant and a Time to Uproot; A History of Agriculture in Papua New Guinea*. Institute of Papua New Guinea Studies.

Flannery Timothy. *Mammals of New Guinea*. Robert Brown and Associates, 1990.

Gressitt JL (ed). *Biogeography and Ecology of New Guinea* (volumes 1 and 2). Dr W Junk, 1982.

Hope GS, Peterson JA, Radok U, Allison I. *The Equatorial Glaciers of New Guinea*. AA Balkema, 1976.

Johnson RW, Threlfall NA. *Volcano Town; The 1937–43 Rabaul Eruptions*. Robert Brown and Associates, 1985.

Leahy Michael, Crain Maurice. *The Land That Time Forgot*. Hurst and Blackett Ltd, 1937.

Mackay Roy D. *New Guinea*. Time-Life Books, 1976.

McAlpine JR, Keig Gael, Falls R. *Climate of Papua New Guinea*. Australian National University Press, 1983.

Menzies JI. *Handbook of Common New Guinea Frogs*. Wau Ecology Institute, Papua New Guinea.

Menzies JI, Dennis Elizabeth. *Handbook of New Guinea Rodents*, Wau Ecology Institute, Papua New Guinea.

Mitton Robert. *The Lost World of Irian Jaya*. Oxford University Press, 1983.

Monbiot George. *Poisoned Arrows; An Investigative Journey Through Indonesia*. Michael Joseph, 1989.

Muller Kal. *Indonesian New Guinea; Irian Jaya*. Periplus Editions Inc., 1990.

O'Hanlon Michael. *Reading the Skin; Adornment, Display and Society among the Wahgi*. British Museum Publications, 1989.

Paijmans K (ed). *New Guinea Vegetation*. Elsevier Scientific, 1976.

Petocz Ronald G. *Conservation and Development in Irian Jaya*. EJ Brill, 1989.

Souter Gavin. *New Guinea; The Last Unknown*. Angus and Robertson Ltd, 1964.

Steene Roger. *Coral Reefs; Nature's Richest Realm*, Charles Letts & Co Ltd, 1990.

Turner Mark. *Papua New Guinea; The Challenge of Independence*. Penguin Books, 1990.

Veron JEN. *Corals of Australia and the Indo-Pacific*. Angus and Robertson Publishers, 1986.

Wheeler Tony. *Papua New Guinea; A Travel Survival Kit*. Lonely Planet Publications, 1988.

INDEX

Figures in italics refer to numbers preceding captions within the colour sections.